THE ULTIMATE

GREEK

PHRASE BOOK

1001 GREEK PHRASES FOR
BEGINNERS AND BEYOND!

BY ADRIAN GEE

ISBN: 979-8-873677-81-8

Copyright © 2024 by Adrian Gee.

All rights reserved.

Author's Note

Welcome to "The Ultimate Greek Phrase Book"! It is my absolute pleasure to guide you through the captivating realms of Greek, a language steeped in ancient history and celebrated for its eloquent beauty and philosophical depth. Whether you are drawn to the mythical echoes of Olympus, the sun-kissed shores of the Aegean, or the rich tapestry of Greek culture and cuisine, this book is meticulously crafted to ensure your journey into Greek language learning is as enriching and delightful as possible.

As a passionate linguist and a fervent advocate for cultural immersion, I appreciate the intricate art of mastering a new language. This book is a culmination of that passion, designed to be your trusted ally on the road to Greek proficiency.

Connect with Me: The journey of language learning goes beyond memorizing words and rules—it's an exciting adventure into building connections and understanding the soul of a culture. I invite you to join me and fellow language enthusiasts on Instagram: @adriangruszka, for a vibrant community where we share knowledge and experiences.

Sharing is Caring: If this book becomes a key part of your language learning journey, I would be deeply honored by your recommendation to others who share a love for the linguistic diversity of our world. Feel free to share your learning milestones or moments of triumph on Instagram, and tag me – I look forward to celebrating each of your achievements!

Embarking on the Greek language is like navigating through a landscape filled with historical richness, enduring traditions, and a sense of communal warmth. Embrace the challenges, celebrate your successes, and cherish every moment of your Greek language adventure.

Καλή τύχη! (Good luck!)

- Adrian Gee

CONTENTS

Introduction... 1
Greetings and Introductions... 9
Eating and Dining.. 27
Travel and Transportation... 43
Accommodations.. 61
Shopping... 75
Emergencies.. 89
Everyday Conversations.. 105
Business and Work.. 119
Events and Entertainment.. 133
Healthcare and Medical Needs..147
Family and Relationships... 161
Technology and Communication.. 173
Sports and Recreation... 187
Transport and Directions... 201
Special Occasions... 215
Conclusion... 227

INTRODUCTION

Kalimera! (Good morning!)

Whether you're picturing yourself wandering through the ancient ruins of Athens, anticipating the taste of fresh olives and feta under the Mediterranean sun, aiming to connect with Greek speakers, or simply drawn to the Greek language with its rich historical and cultural legacy, this phrase book is tailored to be your faithful companion.

Embarking on the journey of learning Greek invites you into a world marked by its profound historical significance, vibrant cultural expressions, and a language that has shaped much of Western thought.

Giati Ellinika? (Why Greek?)

With over 13 million speakers globally, Greek is not only the language of Homer and Plato, the birthplace of democracy, and the cradle of Western civilization, but it is also a vital language in the realms of science, medicine, and the arts. As the official language of Greece and Cyprus, it serves as a key to unlocking the treasures of the Eastern Mediterranean for travelers, scholars, and anyone enchanted by its enduring charm.

Pronoia (Pronunciation)

Before we explore the rich tapestry of phrases and expressions, it is crucial to acquaint yourself with the unique cadence of Greek. Each language has its own rhythm, and Greek flows with a blend of historical depth and contemporary vibrancy. Initially, the distinct sounds and intonations of Greek may seem challenging, but with practice, they can become an exhilarating part of your language learning experience.

Greek pronunciation is characterized by its clarity and variety of sounds, including the soft roll of 'r's and the distinct 'th' sound as in 'θ' (theta). Emphasizing the correct syllables and mastering the melodic intonation not only enhances your communication but also deepens your connection to the rich heritage and welcoming spirit of Greek-speaking communities.

Elliniko Alfabeto (The Greek Alphabet)

The Greek alphabet is one of the oldest writing systems and is distinctive for its rich historical significance. It consists of 24 letters, each with a unique pronunciation that can differ from their English counterparts. Learning these letters is the first step to unlocking the beauty of the Greek language.

Vokalia (Vowels)

A (α - alpha): Like the "a" in "father."
E (ε - epsilon): Similar to the "e" in "bet."
H (η - eta), I (ι - iota), Υ (υ - upsilon): Similar to the "ee" in "see."
O (o - omicron): Like the "o" in "pot."
Ω (ω - omega): Similar to the "o" in "store."

Syggrammata (Consonants)

B (β - beta): Like the "v" in "vine."
Γ (γ - gamma): Before "ε," "η," "ι," "υ," it sounds like the "y" in "yes." Elsewhere, like the "g" in "go."
Δ (δ - delta): Similar to the "th" in "this."
Z (ζ - zeta): Like the "z" in "zebra."
Θ (θ - theta): Similar to the "th" in "think."
K (κ - kappa): Like the "k" in "kite."

Λ (λ - **lambda**): As in English "lion."
M (μ - **mu**): Like the English "m" in "mother."
N (ν - **nu**): Like the "n" in "nice."
Ξ (ξ - **xi**): Similar to "ks" as in "box."
Π (π - **pi**): As in English "pen."
P (ρ - **rho**): A rolling "r," pronounced at the front of the mouth.
Σ (σ/ς - **sigma**): Like the "s" in "see."
T (τ - **tau**): Like the "t" in "top."
Φ (φ - **phi**): Similar to "f" as in "father."
X (χ - **chi**): Similar to the Scottish "loch."
Ψ (ψ - **psi**): Like "ps" in "lapse."

Diplo Syggrammata (Double Letters)

Some sounds in Greek are represented by combinations of letters, such as:

ΓΚ (γκ): Like the "g" in "go."
ΜΠ (μπ): Like the "b" in "ball."
NT (ντ): Similar to the "d" in "dog."

Note that the pronunciation of Greek letters can vary slightly based on their position in a word and the letters surrounding them. This ancient alphabet is the foundation upon which the Greek language has been built, carrying with it centuries of history and culture. Understanding these sounds is essential for delving deeper into the language and its magnificent heritage.

Greek Intonation and Stress Patterns

Greek intonation possesses a unique melody, reflecting the language's long history and cultural richness. In Greek, stress is also crucial and typically falls on one of the last three syllables of a word. This stress can alter the meaning of words, making it a vital aspect of pronunciation to grasp for effective communication.

Common Pronunciation Challenges

Dyskola Dipthonga (Difficult Diphthongs)

Greek features several diphthongs – combinations of two vowels in a single syllable. Mastering these sounds, which often don't have direct equivalents in English, is critical. Additionally, the length of vowel sounds can play a significant role in differentiating word meanings.

Tips for Practicing Pronunciation

1. **Akouste Prosekto (Listen Carefully):** Immersing yourself in Greek through music, podcasts, films, or TV shows is an excellent way to familiarize yourself with the language's rhythm and intonation.

2. **Miliste Meta apo Enan Gennaio (Repeat After a Native Speaker):** Practicing with native speakers, in person or through language exchange apps, can significantly aid in refining your pronunciation.

3. **Chresimopoiete Kathrefti (Use a Mirror):** Watching how your mouth moves can help ensure that your lips, teeth, and tongue are positioned correctly for producing accurate Greek sounds.

4. **Askiste Systimata (Practice Regularly):** Consistent practice, even if it's only a few minutes daily, is crucial for improvement.

5. **Min Fovaste na Kanete Lathi (Don't Fear Mistakes):** Embrace mistakes as a natural and necessary part of the learning process, helping you to understand and improve.

Clear pronunciation is key to effectively navigating the complexities of Greek. Dedicate yourself to mastering the unique sounds, from the harmonious diphthongs to the resonant rolling 'r's, and discover the language that has influenced so many others. Each linguistic nuance captures a fragment of Greece's profound history and vibrant culture. With dedicated practice and an ear attuned to the lyrical flow of Greek, your speech will transcend simple communication, resonating with the depth and beauty of millennia-old traditions.

What You'll Find Inside

*   **Zotika Frasi (Vital Phrases):** A selection of essential sentences and expressions for various situations you might encounter in Greek-speaking environments.

*   **Dialektika Askiseis (Interactive Exercises):** Engaging exercises designed to test and improve your language skills, encouraging active usage of Greek.

*   **Politistikoi Enstikti (Cultural Insights):** Dive into the rich cultural landscape of Greek-speaking regions, from traditional customs to historical landmarks.

*   **Epipleon Poroi (Additional Resources):** A compilation of further materials and advice for enhancing your Greek language skills, including recommended websites, literature, and travel tips.

How to Use This Phrase Book

This book is designed to cater both to beginners embarking on their first exploration of Greek, as well as intermediate learners looking to deepen their fluency. Begin your linguistic journey with essential phrases appropriate for a variety of situations, from casual greetings to navigating the nuances of Greek social customs. As you gain confidence, progress to more intricate language structures and idiomatic expressions that bring you closer to the finesse of a native speaker.

Within these pages, you will find cultural insights that create a deeper connection with Greece's rich history and vibrant contemporary life. Interactive exercises are strategically incorporated to reinforce your learning and help integrate new vocabulary and grammar into your conversations effortlessly.

Learning a language is more than just memorization; it's an engaging, continuous pursuit of connection. Dive into Greek dialogues, explore the nation's celebrated literary heritage, and embrace the customs that weave the fabric of this unique culture.

Every learner's journey to language mastery is unique, characterized by its own pace and milestones. Nurture your skills with patience, enthusiasm, and a spirit of exploration. With dedication, your proficiency and confidence in Greek will not only improve; they will flourish.

Etesi na Arxisete? (Ready to start?)

Embark on a captivating journey into the heart of the Greek language and culture. Uncover its linguistic intricacies and immerse yourself in the cultural richness that Greece offers. This adventure promises to be as rewarding as it is transformative, expanding your horizons and enhancing your global connections.

GREETINGS & INTRODUCTIONS

- BASIC GREETINGS -
- INTRODUCING YOURSELF AND OTHERS -
- EXPRESSING POLITENESS AND FORMALITY -

Basic Greetings

1. Hi!
   Γειά!
   (Yee-ah!)

2. Hello!
   Γεια σας!
   (Yee-ah sahs!)

> **Idiomatic Expression:** "Δεν έχω λόγια." -
> Meaning: "I'm speechless."
> (Literal Translation: "I have no words.")

3. Good morning!
   Καλημέρα!
   (Kah-lee-meh-rah!)

> **Cultural Insight:** Known as 'philoxenia,' Greek
> hospitality is a deeply rooted tradition; guests are treated
> with great warmth and respect.

4. Good afternoon!
   Καλησπέρα!
   (Kah-lee-speh-rah!)

5. Good evening!
   Καλό βράδυ!
   (Kah-loh vrah-dy!)

6. How are you?
   Πώς είσαι;
   (Pohs ee-seh?)

   Cultural Insight: Celebrating one's name day is often considered more important than celebrating one's birthday in Greek culture.

7. Everything good?
   Όλα καλά;
   (Oh-lah kah-lah?)

8. How is it going?
   Πώς πάει;
   (Pohs pah-ee?)

9. How is everything?
   Πώς είναι τα πράγματα;
   (Pohs ee-ne tah prahg-mah-tah?)

10. I'm good, thank you.
    Είμαι καλά, ευχαριστώ.
    (Ee-meh kah-lah, ef-hah-rees-toh.)

11. And you?
    Και εσύ;
    (Keh eh-sy?)

12. Let me introduce...
    Ας συστηθούμε...
    (Ahs see-stee-thoo-meh...)

13. This is...
    Αυτός/Αυτή είναι...
    (Af-tos/Af-tee ee-ne...)

14. Nice to meet you!
Χαίρομαι που σας γνωρίζω!
(Hair-oh-meh poo sas gno-ree-zoh!)

15. Delighted!
Ενθουσιασμένος/η!
(En-thou-siasmé-nos/é!)

16. How have you been?
Πώς έχετε πάει; / Πώς πάει;
(Pós é-he-teh pá-ee?) / (Pós pá-ee?)

Politeness and Formality

17. Excuse me.
Συγγνώμη.
(Seen-yó-mee.)

18. Please.
Παρακαλώ.
(Pa-ra-ka-ló.)

19. Thank you.
Ευχαριστώ.
(Ef-ha-rees-tó.)

> **Fun Fact:** The Greek alphabet was the basis for the Latin, Cyrillic, and several other alphabets.

20. Thank you very much!
Σας ευχαριστώ πάρα πολύ!
(Sas ef-ha-rees-tó pá-ra po-lee!)

21. I'm sorry.
    Λυπάμαι.
    (Lee-pá-meh.)

22. I apologize.
    Ζητώ συγγνώμη.
    (Zee-tó seen-yó-mee.)

23. Sir
    Κύριε
    (Kee-ree-eh)

24. Madam
    Κυρία
    (Kee-ree-ah)

25. Miss
    Δεσποινίς
    (Des-poi-nís)

26. Your name, please?
    Πώς σας λένε;
    (Pós sas lé-ne?)

27. Can I help you with anything?
    Μπορώ να σας βοηθήσω με κάτι;
    (Bo-ró na sas voi-thí-so me ká-ti?)

28. I am thankful for your help.
    Είμαι ευγνώμων για τη βοήθειά σας.
    (Eí-mai ef-gnó-mon gia ti voi-thiá sas.)

29. The pleasure is mine.
    Το κέρδος είναι δικό μου.
    (To kérdos eínai di-kó mou.)

30. Thank you for your hospitality.
Ευχαριστώ για τη φιλοξενία σας.
(Ef-ha-rees-tó yia ti fee-lok-se-nee-a sas.)

31. It's nice to see you again.
Χαίρομαι που σας βλέπω ξανά.
(Hair-oh-meh poo sas vlé-po ksah-ná.)

Greetings for Different Times of Day

32. Good morning, my friend!
Καλημέρα, φίλε μου!
(Kah-lee-mé-ra, fee-le mou!)

33. Good afternoon, colleague!
Καλησπέρα, συνάδελφε!
(Kah-lee-spé-ra, see-ná-thel-fe!)

34. Good evening neighbor!
Καλό βράδυ, γείτονα!
(Kaló vrá-thy, yée-to-na!)

35. Have a good night!
Καλό βράδυ!
(Kaló vrá-thy!)

36. Sleep well!
Καλό ύπνο!
(Kaló éep-no!)

Special Occasions

37. Happy birthday!
Χρόνια πολλά!
(Hró-nee-a po-llá!)

> **Language Learning Tip:** Start with the Alphabet - Familiarize yourself with the Greek alphabet; it's the foundation of the language.

38. Merry Christmas!
Καλά Χριστούγεννα!
(Ka-lá Hree-stoú-yen-na!)

39. Happy Easter!
Καλό Πάσχα!
(Ka-ló Pás-ha!)

> **Travel Story:** In the bustling Athens marketplace, a shopkeeper described his colorful array of spices as "Χίλια δυο χρώματα," meaning "A thousand and two colors," symbolizing their vast variety.

40. Happy holidays!
Καλές γιορτές!
(Ka-lés yor-tés!)

41. Happy New Year!
Καλή Χρονιά!
(Ka-lée Hro-nee-á!)

> **Idiomatic Expression:** "Έβγαλε το λάδι." - Meaning: "Worked very hard."
> (Literal Translation: "Made oil come out.")

Meeting Someone for the First Time

42. Pleasure to meet you.
   Χαίρομαι που σας γνωρίζω.
   (Hair-oh-meh poo sas gno-ree-zoh.)

> **Language Learning Tip:** Use Flashcards - Create flashcards for vocabulary and phrases to reinforce memory.

43. I am [Your Name].
   Είμαι ο/η [Your Name].
   (Ee-meh o/ee [Your Name].)

44. Where are you from?
   Από πού είστε;
   (Apó poo ees-teh?)

> **Language Learning Tip:** Practice Daily - Even a few minutes of practice every day can make a significant difference.

45. I'm on vacation.
   Είμαι σε διακοπές.
   (Ee-meh seh thya-ko-pés.)

46. What is your profession?
   Ποιο είναι το επάγγελμά σας;
   (Pee-o ee-ne to eh-páng-el-ma sas?)

47. How long will you stay here?
Για πόσο καιρό θα μείνετε εδώ;
(Yah pó-so keh-ró tha mee-ne-teh e-thó?)

Responding to Greetings

48. Hello, how have you been?
Γεια σου, πώς είσαι;
(Yia soo, pós ee-sai?)

> **Cultural Insight:** Traditional Greek coffee is strong and served with the grounds in the cup. It's often enjoyed slowly, with friends.

49. I've been very busy lately.
Έχω απασχοληθεί πολύ τελευταία.
(É-ho a-pas-cho-lee-theí po-lí te-lef-té-a.)

50. I've had ups and downs.
Έχω ζήσει σκαμπανεβάσματα.
(É-ho zée-see skam-pa-ne-vás-ma-ta.)

> **Idiomatic Expression:** "Έχω πολλά στο πιάτο μου." - Meaning: "I have a lot on my plate (very busy)." (Literal Translation: "I have a lot on my plate.")

51. Thanks for asking.
Ευχαριστώ που ρωτάτε.
(Ef-ha-rees-tó poo ro-tá-te.)

52. I feel great.
Αισθάνομαι υπέροχα.
(Ees-thá-no-meh ee-pér-o-ha.)

53. Life has been good.
Η ζωή ήταν καλή.
(Ee zo-ée ée-tan ka-lée.)

54. I can't complain.
Δεν μπορώ να παραπονεθώ.
(Den bo-ró na pa-ra-po-ne-thó.)

55. And you, how are you?
Και εσύ, πώς είσαι;
(Keh esý, pós ee-sai?)

Language Learning Tip: Listen to Greek Music - Music can help with pronunciation and cultural immersion.

56. I've had some challenges.
Αντιμετώπισα κάποιες προκλήσεις.
(An-tee-me-tó-pee-sa ká-pyees pro-klí-sees.)

57. Life is a journey.
Η ζωή είναι ένα ταξίδι.
(Ee zo-ée ee-ne é-na tak-sí-dee.)

58. Thank God, I'm fine.
Ευχαριστώ το Θεό, είμαι καλά.
(Ef-ha-rees-tó to Theó, ee-meh ka-lá.)

Informal Greetings

59. What's up?
Τι κάνεις;
(Tee ká-nees?)

60. All good?
Όλα καλά;
(Ó-la ka-lá?)

61. Hi, everything okay?
Γειά, όλα καλά;
(Yiá, ó-la ka-lá?)

62. I'm good, and you?
Είμαι καλά, εσύ;
(Ee-meh ka-lá, esý?)

63. How's life?
Πώς πάει η ζωή;
(Pós pá-ee ee zo-ée?)

64. Cool!
Τέλειο!
(Té-lei-o!)

Saying Goodbye

65. Goodbye!
Αντίο!
(An-tí-o!)

66. See you later!
Τα λέμε αργότερα!
(Ta lé-me ar-gó-te-ra!)

> **Language Learning Tip:** Watch Greek Movies -
> Watching movies in Greek enhances listening skills and
> cultural understanding.

67. Bye!
Γειά!
(Yiá!)

68. Have a good day.
Καλή μέρα.
(Ka-lée mé-ra.)

> **Language Learning Tip:** Use Language Apps - Apps like
> Duolingo, Babbel, or Rosetta Stone can be effective tools
> for learning.

69. Have a good weekend.
Καλό σαββατοκύριακο.
(Ka-ló sav-va-to-kí-ri-a-ko.)

70. Take care.
Να προσέχεις.
(Na pro-sé-heis.)

71. Bye, see you later.
Γειά, τα λέμε αργότερα.
(Yiá, ta lé-me ar-gó-te-ra.)

72. I need to go now.
Πρέπει να φύγω τώρα.
(Pré-pei na fí-go tó-ra.)

73. Take care my friend!
Να προσέχεις, φίλε μου!
(Na pro-sé-heis, fí-le mou!)

Parting Words

74. Hope to see you soon.
Ελπίζω να σε δω σύντομα.
(El-pí-zo na se do sí-nto-ma.)

75. Stay in touch.
Να επικοινωνούμε.
(Na e-pi-ko-i-no-nóu-me.)

76. I'll miss you.
Θα μου λείψεις.
(Tha mou líp-seis.)

77. Be well.
Να είσαι καλά.
(Na í-se ka-lá.)

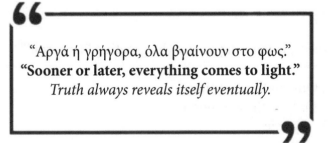

"Αργά ή γρήγορα, όλα βγαίνουν στο φως."
"Sooner or later, everything comes to light."
Truth always reveals itself eventually.

Interactive Challenge: Greetings Quiz

1. How do you say "good morning" in Greek?

   a) Τι κάνεις;
   b) Καλημέρα!
   c) Πώς είσαι;

2. What does the Greek phrase "Χαίρομαι που σε γνώρισα" mean in English?

   a) Excuse me!
   b) Pleased to meet you!
   c) How are you?

3. When is it appropriate to use the phrase "Καλησπέρα!" in Greek?

   a) In the morning
   b) In the afternoon
   c) In the evening

4. Which phrase is used to ask someone how they are doing in Greek?

   a) Ευχαριστώ
   b) Πώς είσαι;
   c) Πού πας;

5. In Greece, when can you use the greeting "Γειά σου!"?

   a) Only in the morning
   b) Only in the afternoon
   c) Anytime

6. What is the Greek equivalent of "And you?"?

   a) Και εσύ;
   b) Ευχαριστώ
   c) Τι κάνεις;

7. When expressing gratitude in Greek, what do you say?

   a) Συγγνώμη
   b) Χαίρομαι που σε γνώρισα
   c) Ευχαριστώ

8. How do you say "Excuse me" in Greek?

   a) Συγγνώμη
   b) Καλό απόγευμα!
   c) Όλα καλά;

9. Which phrase is used to inquire about someone's well-being?

   a) Πού μένεις;
   b) Πώς είσαι;
   c) Ευχαριστώ

10. In a typical Greek conversation, when is it common to ask about someone's background and interests during a first-time meeting?

    a) Never
    b) Only in formal situations
    c) Always

11. In Greek, what does "Χαίρομαι που σε γνώρισα" mean?

a) Delighted to meet you
b) Excuse me
c) Thank you

12. When should you use the phrase "Πώς είσαι;"?

a) When ordering food
b) When asking for directions
c) When inquiring about someone's well-being

13. Which phrase is used to make requests politely?

a) Πώς είσαι;
b) Τι θέλεις;
c) Παρακαλώ

14. What is the equivalent of "I'm sorry" in Greek?

a) Λυπάμαι
b) Πώς είσαι;
c) Όλα καλά

Correct Answers:

1. b)
2. b)
3. c)
4. b)
5. c)
6. a)
7. c)
8. a)
9. b)
10. c)
11. a)
12. c)
13. c)
14. a)

EATING & DINING

- ORDERING FOOD AND DRINKS IN A RESTAURANT -
- DIETARY PREFERENCES AND RESTRICTIONS -
- COMPLIMENTS AND COMPLAINTS ABOUT FOOD -

Basic Ordering

78. I'd like a table for two, please.
Θα ήθελα ένα τραπέζι για δύο, παρακαλώ.
(Tha í-thela é-na tra-pé-zi yia dýo, pa-ra-ka-ló.)

79. What's the special of the day?
Ποιο είναι το ειδικό της ημέρας;
(Pee-o ee-ne to ee-di-kó tis i-mé-ras?)

> **Cultural Insight:** Traditional dances, often in a circle, are an integral part of Greek culture, expressing joy and community spirit.

80. Can I see the menu, please?
Μπορώ να δω τον κατάλογο, παρακαλώ;
(Bo-ró na do ton ka-tá-lo-go, pa-ra-ka-ló?)

81. I'll have the steak, medium rare.
Θα πάρω μπριζόλα, μέτρια ψημένη.
(Tha pá-ro bree-zó-la, mé-tria psee-mé-nee.)

82. Can I get a glass of water?
Μπορώ να έχω ένα ποτήρι νερό, παρακαλώ;
(Bo-ró na é-ho é-na po-tí-ri ne-ró, pa-ra-ka-ló?)

> **Travel Story:** While watching the sunset in Santorini, a local said, "Όπου κι αν πας, εκεί είσαι," meaning "Wherever you go, there you are," reflecting on the beauty of the present moment.

33. Can you bring us some bread to start?
Μπορείτε να μας φέρετε λίγο ψωμί για αρχή;
(Bo-ree-te na mas fé-re-te lí-go pso-mí yia ar-hí?)

34. Do you have a vegetarian option?
Έχετε βεγεταριανή επιλογή;
(É-he-te ve-ge-ta-ri-a-ní e-pi-lo-gí?)

> **Language Learning Tip:** Label Household Items - Place labels on everyday items around your home in Greek.

35. Is there a kids' menu available?
Έχετε μενού για παιδιά;
(É-he-te me-noú yia pe-di-á?)

36. We'd like to order appetizers to share.
Θέλουμε να παραγγείλουμε ορεκτικά για να μοιραστούμε.
(Thé-lou-me na pa-ran-gee-í-lou-me o-rek-ti-ká yia na mee-ras-tóu-me.)

37. Can we have separate checks, please?
Μπορούμε να έχουμε ξεχωριστούς λογαριασμούς, παρακαλώ;
(Bo-róu-me na é-hou-me xe-ho-ri-stoús lo-ga-ri-a-smoús, pa-ra-ka-ló?)

38. Could you recommend a vegetarian dish?
Μπορείτε να μου προτείνετε ένα βεγεταριανό πιάτο;
(Bo-ree-te na mou pro-tí-ne-te é-na ve-ge-ta-ri-a-nó piá-to?)

39. I'd like to try the local cuisine.
Θα ήθελα να δοκιμάσω την τοπική κουζίνα.
(Tha í-thela na do-ki-má-so tin to-pi-kí kou-zí-na.)

90. May I have a refill on my drink, please?
Μπορώ να ξαναγεμίσω το ποτό μου, παρακαλώ;
(Bo-ró na ksa-na-ye-mí-so to po-tó mou, pa-ra-ka-ló?)

91. What's the chef's special today?
Ποιο είναι το σημερινό ειδικό πιάτο του σεφ;
(Pee-o ee-ne to see-me-ri-nó ee-di-kó pee-á-to tou sef?)

92. Can you make it extra spicy?
Μπορείτε να το κάνετε πιο πικάντικο, παρακαλώ;
(Bo-ree-te na to ká-ne-te pee-o pee-kán-ti-ko, pa-ra-ka-ló?)

93. I'll have the chef's tasting menu.
Θα πάρω το δοκιμαστικό μενού του σεφ.
(Tha pá-ro to do-ki-mas-ti-kó me-noú tou sef.)

Special Requests

94. I'm allergic to nuts. Is this dish nut-free?
Είμαι αλλεργικός/ή στα καρύδια. Είναι αυτό το πιάτο χωρίς καρύδια;
(Ee-meh a-le-rgi-kós/ή sta ka-rý-dia. Ee-ne af-tó to pee-á-to ho-rís ka-rý-dia?)

95. I'm on a gluten-free diet. What can I have?
Κάνω δίαιτα χωρίς γλουτένη. Τι μπορώ να πάρω;
(Ká-no thí-e-ta ho-rís glou-té-ni. Ti bo-ró na pá-ro?)

96. Can you make it less spicy, please?
Μπορείτε να το κάνετε λιγότερο πικάντικο, παρακαλώ;
(Bo-ree-te na to ká-ne-te li-gó-te-ro pee-kán-ti-ko, pa-ra-ka-ló?)

Idiomatic Expression: "Θα φάω το κεφάλι μου." -
Meaning: "I'm really frustrated or worried."
(Literal translation: "I will eat my head.")

97. Can you recommend a local specialty?
Μπορείτε να προτείνετε κάποιο τοπικό ειδικό πιάτο;
(Bo-ree-te na pro-tí-ne-te ká-py-o to-pi-kó ee-di-kó pee-á-to?)

98. Could I have my salad without onions?
Μπορώ να έχω τη σαλάτα μου χωρίς κρεμμύδια;
(Bo-ró na é-ho ti sa-lá-ta mou ho-rís kre-mý-dia?)

99. Are there any daily specials?
Έχετε κανένα σημερινό ειδικό πιάτο;
(É-he-te ka-né-na see-me-ri-nó ee-di-kó pee-á-to?)

Fun Fact: The first recorded Olympic Games were held in Olympia, Greece in 776 BC.

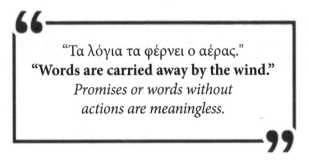

"Τα λόγια τα φέρνει ο αέρας."
"Words are carried away by the wind."
*Promises or words without
actions are meaningless.*

100.   Can I get a side of extra sauce?
       Μπορώ να έχω λίγη επιπλέον σάλτσα, παρακαλώ;
       (Bo-ró na é-ho lí-gi e-pi-plé-on sál-tsa, pa-ra-ka-ló?)

101.   I'd like a glass of red/white wine, please.
       Θα ήθελα ένα ποτήρι κόκκινο/λευκό κρασί, παρακαλώ.
       (Tha í-thela é-na po-tí-ri kók-ki-no/lef-kó kra-sí, pa-ra-ka-ló.)

102.   Could you bring the bill, please?
       Μπορείτε να μου φέρετε τον λογαριασμό, παρακαλώ;
       (Bo-ree-te na mou fé-re-te ton lo-ga-ri-as-mó, pa-ra-ka-ló?)

Allergies and Intolerances

103.   I have a dairy allergy. Is the sauce dairy-free?
       **Έχω αλλεργία στα γαλακτοκομικά. Είναι η σάλτσα χωρίς
       γαλακτοκομικά;**
       *(É-ho a-le-rghí-a sta ga-lak-to-ko-mi-ká. Eí-nai ee sál-tsa ho-rís
       ga-lak-to-ko-mi-ká?)*

104.   Does this contain any seafood? I have an allergy.
       Περιέχει αυτό θαλασσινά; Έχω αλλεργία.
       (Pe-rié-hi af-tó tha-las-si-ná? É-ho a-le-rghí-a.)

105.   I can't eat anything with soy. Is that an issue?
       Δεν μπορώ να τρώω τίποτα με σόγια. Υπάρχει πρόβλημα;
       (Den bo-ró na tró-o tí-po-ta me só-yia. I-pár-hi pró-vli-ma?)

106. I'm lactose intolerant, so no dairy, please.
Έχω δυσανεξία στη λακτόζη, οπότε παρακαλώ χωρίς
γαλακτοκομικά.
*(É-ho dy-san-exí-a sti lak-tó-zi, o-pó-te pa-ra-ka-ló ho-rís
ga-lak-to-ko-mi-ká.)*

107. Is there an option for those with nut allergies?
Υπάρχει επιλογή για αυτούς με αλλεργία στους καρπούς;
(I-pár-hi e-pi-lo-gí yia af-toús me a-le-rghí-a stous kar-poús?)

108. I'm following a vegan diet. Is that possible?
Ακολουθώ μια vegan διατροφή. Είναι εφικτό;
(A-ko-lo-thó mia vegan di-a-tro-fí. Eí-nai e-fi-któ?)

> **Fun Fact:** Greece has one of the longest coastlines in the
> world, about 13,676 km.

109. Is this dish suitable for someone with allergies?
Είναι αυτό το πιάτο κατάλληλο για κάποιον με αλλεργίες;
(Eí-nai af-tó to pi-á-to ka-tál-li-lo yia ká-py-on me a-le-rghí-es?)

110. I'm trying to avoid dairy. Any dairy-free options?
Προσπαθώ να αποφύγω τα γαλακτοκομικά. Υπάρχουν
επιλογές χωρίς γαλακτοκομικά;
*(Pro-spa-thó na a-po-fí-go ta ga-lak-to-ko-mi-ká. I-pár-houn
e-pi-lo-gés ho-rís ga-lak-to-ko-mi-ká?)*

111. I have a shellfish allergy. Is it safe to order seafood?
Έχω αλλεργία στα οστρακοειδή. Είναι ασφαλές να
παραγγείλω θαλασσινά;
*(É-ho a-le-rghí-a sta os-tra-ko-ei-dí. Eí-nai as-fa-lés na
pa-ran-gí-lo tha-las-si-ná?)*

112. Can you make this gluten-free?
Μπορείτε να το κάνετε χωρίς γλουτένη;
(Bo-ree-te na to ká-ne-te ho-rís glou-té-ni?)

> **Language Learning Tip:** Practice with Native Speakers - Conversation with native speakers is invaluable for practical learning.

Specific Dietary Requests

113. I prefer my food without cilantro.
Προτιμώ το φαγητό μου χωρίς κολίανδρο.
(Pro-ti-mó to fa-yi-tó mou ho-rís ko-lí-an-dro.)

114. Could I have the dressing on the side?
Μπορώ να έχω τη σάλτσα χωριστά;
(Bo-ró na é-ho ti sál-tsa ho-ri-stá?)

115. Can you make it vegan-friendly?
Μπορείτε να το κάνετε vegan;
(Bo-ree-te na to ká-ne-te vegan?)

116. I'd like extra vegetables with my main course.
Θα ήθελα επιπλέον λαχανικά με το κυρίως πιάτο.
(Tha í-thela e-pi-plé-on la-ha-ni-ká me to kyrí-os pee-á-to.)

117. Is this suitable for someone on a keto diet?
Είναι αυτό κατάλληλο για κάποιον που κάνει κετο διατροφή;
(Eí-nai af-tó ka-tál-li-lo yia ká-py-on pou ká-nei keto di-a-tro-fí?)

118. I prefer my food with less oil, please.
      Προτιμώ το φαγητό μου με λιγότερο λάδι, παρακαλώ.
      (Pro-ti-mó to fa-yi-tó mou me li-gó-te-ro lá-di, pa-ra-ka-ló.)

119. Is this dish suitable for vegetarians?
      Είναι αυτό το πιάτο κατάλληλο για χορτοφάγους;
      (Eí-nai af-tó to pee-á-to ka-tál-li-lo yia hor-to-fá-gous?)

120. I'm on a low-carb diet. What would you recommend?
      Κάνω δίαιτα με λίγους υδατάνθρακες. Τι θα προτείνατε;
      (Ká-no dí-ai-ta me lí-gous y-da-tán-thra-kes. Ti tha pro-tí-na-te?)

> **Fun Fact:** The long-distance race, the marathon,
> originated in Greece, commemorating the run of the
> soldier Pheidippides from the Battle of Marathon to
> Athens.

121. Is the bread here gluten-free?
      Είναι το ψωμί εδώ χωρίς γλουτένη;
      (Eí-nai to pso-mí e-thó ho-rís glou-té-ni?)

122. I'm watching my sugar intake. Any sugar-free desserts?
      Προσέχω την πρόσληψη ζάχαρης. Υπάρχουν γλυκά χωρίς
      ζάχαρη;
      *(Pro-sé-ho tin pró-slip-si zá-ha-ris. I-pár-houn gly-ká ho-rís
      zá-ha-ri?)*

> **Travel Story:** In the ancient ruins of Delphi, a guide
> quoted "Πάν μέτρον άριστον," translating to "Everything
> in moderation," a principle of balanced living.

Compliments

123.   This meal is delicious!
Το φαγητό είναι νόστιμο!
(To fa-yi-tó ee-ne nó-sti-mo!)

> **Fun Fact:** Ancient Greece is often called the birthplace of Western philosophy, with thinkers like Socrates, Plato, and Aristotle.

124.   The flavors in this dish are amazing.
Οι γεύσεις σε αυτό το πιάτο είναι εκπληκτικές.
(Oi gév-sis se af-tó to pi-á-to ee-ne ek-plek-ti-kés.)

125.   I love the presentation of the food.
Λατρεύω την παρουσίαση του φαγητού.
(La-tre-vó tin pa-rou-sí-a-si tou fa-yi-toú.)

126.   This dessert is outstanding!
Το γλυκό είναι εξαιρετικό!
(To gly-kó ee-ne ex-er-re-ti-kó!)

127.   The service here is exceptional.
Η εξυπηρέτηση εδώ είναι εξαιρετική.
(Ee ex-y-per-é-ti-si e-thó ee-ne ex-er-re-ti-kí.)

> **Language Learning Tip:** Record Your Voice - Record and listen to yourself to improve your pronunciation.

128.   The chef deserves praise for this dish.
Ο σεφ αξίζει έπαινος για αυτό το πιάτο.
(O sef axí-zei é-pe-nos yia af-tó to pi-á-to.)

129. I'm impressed by the quality of the ingredients.
Εντυπωσιάστηκα από την ποιότητα των συστατικών.
(En-di-po-siás-ti-ka apó tin pi-ó-ti-ta ton sys-ta-ti-kón.)

130. The atmosphere in this restaurant is wonderful.
Η ατμόσφαιρα σε αυτό το εστιατόριο είναι υπέροχη.
(Ee at-mós-fe-ra se af-tó to es-ti-a-tó-rio ee-ne é-pé-ro-hi.)

131. Everything we ordered was perfect.
Όλα όσα παραγγείλαμε ήταν τέλεια.
(Ó-la ó-sa pa-ran-gí-la-me í-tan té-le-ia.)

Compaints

132. The food is cold. Can you reheat it?
Το φαγητό είναι κρύο. Μπορείτε να το ξαναζεστάνετε;
(To fa-yi-tó ee-ne krí-o. Bo-ree-te na to ksa-na-zes-tá-ne-te?)

> **Fun Fact:** About 25% of the English vocabulary comes from Greek words.

133. This dish is too spicy for me.
Αυτό το πιάτο είναι πολύ πικάντικο για μένα.
(Af-tó to pi-á-to ee-ne po-lí pi-kán-ti-ko yia mé-na.)

134. The portion size is quite small.
Το μέγεθος της μερίδας είναι αρκετά μικρό.
(To mé-ge-thos tis me-rí-das ee-ne ar-ke-tá mi-kró.)

135.   There's a hair in my food.
       Υπάρχει τρίχα στο φαγητό μου.
       (I-pár-hi trí-ha sto fa-yi-tó mou.)

136.   I'm not satisfied with the service.
       Δεν είμαι ικανοποιημένος/η με την εξυπηρέτηση.
       (Den ee-me i-ka-no-poi-i-mé-nos/ni me tin ex-y-per-é-ti-si.)

137.   The soup is lukewarm.
       Η σούπα είναι χλιαρή.
       (Ee soú-pa ee-ne hlia-rí.)

138.   The sauce on this dish is too salty.
       Η σάλτσα σε αυτό το πιάτο είναι πολύ αλμυρή.
       (Ee sál-tsa se af-tó to pi-á-to ee-ne po-lí al-my-rí.)

              Idiomatic Expression: "Κάνω τα στραβά μάτια."
              Meaning: "Turn a blind eye."
              (Literal translation: "I make my eyes crooked.")

139.   The dessert was a bit disappointing.
       Το γλυκό ήταν λίγο απογοητευτικό.
       (To gly-kó í-tan lí-go a-po-goi-tef-ti-kó.)

140.   I ordered this dish, but you brought me something else.
       Παρήγγειλα αυτό το πιάτο, αλλά μου φέρατε κάτι άλλο.
       (Pa-rín-gi-la af-tó to pi-á-to, al-lá mou fé-ra-te ká-ti ál-lo.)

141.   The food took a long time to arrive.
       Το φαγητό άργησε να έρθει.
       (To fa-yi-tó ár-gi-se na ér-thi.)

Specific Dish Feedback

142. The steak is overcooked.
Το μπριζόλα είναι υπερβρασμένο.
(To bri-zó-la ee-ne y-per-vra-s mé-no.)

> **Fun Fact:** Greece has over 6,000 islands, though only around 227 are inhabited.

143. This pasta is undercooked.
Αυτή η πάστα είναι λίγο ανώμαλη.
(Af-tí ee pás-ta ee-ne lí-go a-nó-ma-li.)

144. The fish tastes off. Is it fresh?
Το ψάρι έχει περίεργη γεύση. Είναι φρέσκο;
(To psá-ri é-hi pe-rí-er-gi géf-si. Eí-nai frés-ko?)

145. The salad dressing is too sweet.
Η σάλτσα της σαλάτας είναι πολύ γλυκιά.
(Ee sál-tsa tis sa-lá-tas ee-ne po-lí gly-kiá.)

146. The rice is underseasoned.
Το ρύζι είναι ανοστο.
(To rí-zi ee-ne a-nos-to.)

> **Language Learning Tip:** Set Realistic Goals - Setting achievable goals keeps you motivated and structured.

147. The dessert lacks flavor.
Το γλυκό λείπει από γεύση.
(To gly-kó lí-pi a-pó géf-si.)

148.   The vegetables are overcooked.
        Τα λαχανικά είναι υπερβρασμένα.
        (Ta la-ha-ni-ká ee-ne y-per-vra-s mé-na.)

149.   The pizza crust is burnt.
        Η πίτσα έχει καεί στην κόρα.
        (Ee pít-sa é-hi ke-í stin kó-ra.)

        Travel Story: At a Cretan winery, the vintner raised a
        glass and said, "Στην υγειά μας," meaning "To our
        health," a common Greek toast.

150.   The burger is dry.
        Το μπέργκερ είναι στεγνό.
        (To bé-rger ee-ne ste-gnó.)

151.   The fries are too greasy.
        Οι πατάτες τηγανιτές είναι πολύ λιπαρές.
        (Oi pa-tá-tes ti-ya-ni-tés ee-ne po-lí li-pa-rés.)

152.   The soup is too watery.
        Η σούπα είναι πολύ νερουλή.
        (Ee soú-pa ee-ne po-lí ne-rou-lí.)

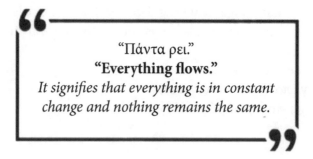

"Πάντα ρει."
"Everything flows."
It signifies that everything is in constant
change and nothing remains the same.

Word Search Puzzle: Eating & Dining

RESTAURANT
ΕΣΤΙΑΤΌΡΙΟ
MENU
ΜΕΝΟΎ
APPETIZER
ΟΡΕΚΤΙΚΌ
VEGETARIAN
ΧΟΡΤΟΦΆΓΟΣ
ALLERGY
ΑΛΛΕΡΓΊΑ
VEGAN
ΒΕΓΚΆΝ
SPECIAL
ΕΙΔΙΚΌ
DESSERT
ΕΠΙΔΌΡΠΙΟ
SERVICE
ΕΞΥΠΗΡΈΤΗΣΗ
CHEF
ΣΕΦ
INGREDIENTS
ΣΥΣΤΑΤΙΚΆ
ATMOSPHERE
ΑΤΜΌΣΦΑΙΡΑ
PERFECT
ΤΈΛΕΙΟς

N	R	D	B	R	F	Q	A	G	E	G	T	F	S	C
G	A	V	E	W	M	L	Q	V	S	C	L	R	H	M
O	R	G	H	S	L	Z	V	Y	E	I	E	C	V	K
V	Z	J	E	E	S	L	G	F	Y	S	J	I	K	T
A	M	Z	R	V	A	E	R	E	T	I	X	D	C	S
E	W	G	Q	I	F	E	R	A	O	X	Q	Z	O	N
V	Y	V	C	B	P	E	U	T	U	G	V	V	Y	A
W	E	E	I	N	G	R	E	D	I	E	N	T	S	K
I	P	G	G	F	A	E	I	Δ	I	K	Ό	V	C	Γ
S	E	F	E	N	O	I	P	Ό	T	A	I	T	Σ	E
N	Π	E	T	T	Φ	N	V	E	M	B	V	I	C	B
T	I	H	P	E	A	H	N	P	B	M	T	C	S	Q
A	Δ	C	Σ	X	T	R	O	J	O	K	Z	X	E	O
Ύ	Ό	K	A	O	M	S	I	V	I	C	Z	Q	V	F
O	P	C	P	P	O	U	P	A	T	H	R	F	I	G
N	Π	N	I	T	S	M	E	T	N	Z	C	U	S	K
E	I	X	A	O	P	U	O	P	E	K	T	I	K	Ό
M	O	W	Φ	Φ	H	G	N	G	P	G	E	Z	W	R
H	X	B	Σ	A	E	T	N	E	R	F	N	L	Y	Z
S	Σ	A	Ό	Γ	R	S	C	E	M	U	M	H	E	L
A	A	H	M	O	E	G	Z	J	V	U	Z	L	Q	F
B	Σ	W	T	Σ	I	I	A	Ί	Γ	P	E	Λ	Λ	A
P	H	Y	A	Έ	T	M	Y	Y	U	A	P	G	O	N
L	X	R	Σ	E	P	E	S	S	O	L	J	S	F	S
B	N	J	P	T	P	H	R	I	M	M	X	K	E	Z
S	O	P	X	M	A	H	Π	Y	F	O	Q	R	N	O
S	A	T	V	I	J	T	H	Y	L	O	V	C	H	D
T	Έ	Λ	E	I	O	Σ	I	G	Ξ	I	M	Q	S	B
W	J	O	O	C	T	B	M	K	C	E	D	W	Z	V
Q	Y	D	I	F	U	L	U	E	A	G	S	B	E	P

Correct Answers:

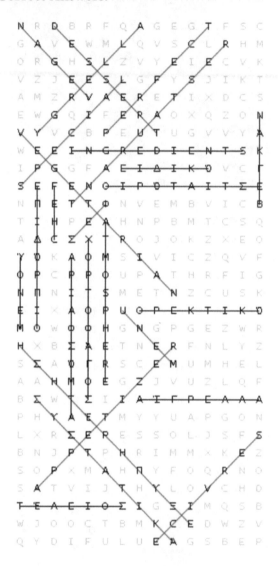

TRAVEL & TRANSPORTATION

- ASKING FOR DIRECTIONS -
- BUYING TICKETS FOR TRANSPORTATION -
- INQUIRING ABOUT TRAVEL-RELATED INFORMATION -

Directions

153.   How do I get to the nearest bus stop?
Πώς μπορώ να βρω την πιο κοντινή στάση λεωφορείου;
(Pós bo-ró na vró tin pio kon-ti-ní stá-si le-o-fo-reí-ou?)

> **Fun Fact:** Greek coffee was traditionally made in a small pot called a 'briki'.

154.   Can you show me the way to the train station?
Μπορείτε να μου δείξετε τον δρόμο για τον σταθμό τρένου;
(Bo-ree-te na mou dí-xe-te ton dró-mo yia ton sta-thmó tré-nou?)

155.   Is there a map of the city center?
Υπάρχει χάρτης του κέντρου της πόλης;
(I-pár-hi hártis tou kén-trou tis pó-lis?)

156.   Which street leads to the airport?
Ποια οδός οδηγεί στο αεροδρόμιο;
(Pia o-dós o-di-ghí sto ae-ro-dró-mio?)

157.   Where is the nearest taxi stand?
Πού είναι η πιο κοντινή στάση ταξί;
(Poú ee-ne ee pio kon-ti-ní stá-si tak-sí?)

> **Travel Story:** In a Thessaloniki café, a patron shared a story, ending with "Το ένα χέρι νίβει το άλλο," which means "One hand washes the other," emphasizing mutual help.

158. How can I find the hotel from here?
Πώς μπορώ να βρω το ξενοδοχείο από εδώ;
(Pós bo-ró na vró to kse-no-do-hí-o apó e-dó?)

> **Fun Fact:** Greece produces about 17% of the world's olive supply.

159. What's the quickest route to the museum?
Ποια είναι η ταχύτερη διαδρομή για το μουσείο;
(Pia ee-ne ee ta-hí-te-ri di-a-dro-mí yia to mou-sí-o?)

160. Is there a pedestrian path to the beach?
Υπάρχει πεζοδρόμιο προς την παραλία;
(I-pár-hi pe-zo-dró-mio pros tin pa-ra-lí-a?)

161. Can you point me towards the city square?
Μπορείτε να με κατευθύνετε προς την πλατεία της πόλης;
(Bo-ree-te na me ka-tef-thí-ne-te pros tin pla-tí-a tis pó-lis?)

> **Idiomatic Expression:** "Κολλάω σαν τσίχλα." - Meaning: "To stick around like glue."
> (Literal translation: "Stick like gum.")

162. How do I find the trailhead for the hiking trail?
Πώς μπορώ να βρω την αρχή του μονοπατιού για πεζοπορία;
(Pós bo-ró na vró tin ar-hí tou mo-no-pa-ti-ú yia pe-zo-po-rí-a?)

> **Fun Fact:** Greek yogurt is known worldwide for its creamy texture and is thicker than regular yogurt.

Ticket Purchase

163. How much is a one-way ticket to downtown?
Πόσο κοστίζει ένα εισιτήριο μονής διαδρομής για το κέντρο;
(Pó-so kos-tí-zei é-na ei-si-tí-rio mo-nís di-a-dro-mís yia to kén-tro?)

164. Are there any discounts for students?
Υπάρχουν έκπτωσεις για φοιτητές;
(I-pár-houn ék-p-to-seis yia fí-ti-tés?)

> **Language Learning Tip:** Be Patient with Yourself -
> Language learning is a process, and it's okay to make
> mistakes.

165. What's the price of a monthly bus pass?
Πόσο κοστίζει μια μηνιαία κάρτα λεωφορείου;
(Pó-so kos-tí-zei mi-a mi-ni-é-a kár-ta le-o-fo-reí-ou?)

166. Can I buy a metro ticket for a week?
Μπορώ να αγοράσω εισιτήριο μετρό για μια εβδομάδα;
(Bo-ró na a-go-rá-so ei-si-tí-rio me-tró yia mi-a ev-do-má-da?)

167. How do I get a refund for a canceled flight?
Πώς μπορώ να πάρω επιστροφή για ακυρωμένη πτήση;
(Pós bo-ró na pá-ro e-pis-tro-fí yia a-ky-ro-mé-ni ptí-si?)

> **Fun Fact:** The first capital of modern Greece was
> Nafplio, before it moved to Athens.

168. Is it cheaper to purchase tickets online or at the station?
Είναι φθηνότερο να αγοράσεις εισιτήρια online ή στον σταθμό;
(Eí-nai fthi-nó-te-ro na a-go-rá-sis ei-si-tí-ria online í ston sta-thmó?)

169. Can I upgrade my bus ticket to first class?
Μπορώ να αναβαθμίσω το εισιτήριο λεωφορείου μου σε πρώτη θέση;
(Bo-ró na a-na-va-thmí-so to ei-si-tí-rio le-o-fo-reí-ou mou se pró-ti thé-si?)

170. Are there any promotions for weekend train travel?
Υπάρχουν προσφορές για ταξίδια με τρένο τα σαββατοκύριακα;
(I-pár-houn pro-sfo-rés yia ta-xí-di-a me tré-no ta sav-va-to-kí-ri-a-ka?)

171. Is there a night bus to the city center?
Υπάρχει νυχτερινό λεωφορείο για το κέντρο;
(I-pár-hi ni-h-te-ri-nó le-o-fo-reí-o yia to kén-tro?)

> **Idiomatic Expression:** "Μου έκατσε στο λαιμό." -
> Meaning: "It stuck in my throat (something bothers me a lot)."
> (Literal translation: "It sat in my throat.")

172. What's the cost of a one-day tram pass?
Πόσο κοστίζει μια ημερήσια κάρτα τραμ;
(Pó-so kos-tí-zei mi-a i-me-rí-sia kár-ta tram?)

> **Fun Fact:** The Greek language has a recorded history of over 3,400 years, making it one of the oldest languages still in use.

Travel Info

173. What's the weather forecast for tomorrow?
Ποια είναι η πρόγνωση καιρού για αύριο;
(Pee-a ee-ne ee pró-gno-si ke-rou yia á-vri-o?)

174. Are there any guided tours of the historical sites?
Υπάρχουν οργανωμένες ξεναγήσεις των ιστορικών μνημείων;
(I-pár-houn or-ga-no-mé-nes kse-na-ghí-seis ton is-to-ri-kón mní-me-ion?)

175. Can you recommend a good local restaurant for dinner?
Μπορείτε να μου προτείνετε ένα καλό τοπικό εστιατόριο για δείπνο;
(Bo-ree-te na mou pro-tí-ne-te é-na ka-ló to-pi-kó es-ti-a-tó-rio yia díp-no?)

176. How do I get to the famous landmarks in town?
Πώς μπορώ να φτάσω στα διάσημα αξιοθέατα της πόλης;
(Pós bo-ró na ftá-so sta diá-si-ma ax-ió-the-a-ta tis pó-lis?)

177. Is there a visitor center at the airport?
Υπάρχει κέντρο επισκεπτών στο αεροδρόμιο;
(I-pár-hi kén-tro e-pi-skep-tón sto ae-ro-dró-mio?)

178. What's the policy for bringing pets on the train?
Ποια είναι η πολιτική για τη μεταφορά κατοικίδιων στο τρένο;
(Pee-a ee-ne ee po-li-ti-kí yia ti me-ta-fo-rá ka-toi-kí-di-on sto tré-no?)

179. Are there any discounts for disabled travelers?
Υπάρχουν έκπτωσεις για ταξιδιώτες με αναπηρία;
(I-pár-houn ék-p-to-seis yia tak-si-di-ó-tes me a-na-pi-rí-a?)

> **Idiomatic Expression:** "Μου καίγονται τα χείλη." -
> Meaning: "It's burning my lips (eager to say something)."
> (Literal translation: "My lips are burning.")

180. Can you provide information about local festivals?
Μπορείτε να μου δώσετε πληροφορίες για τοπικά φεστιβάλ;
(Bo-ree-te na mou dó-se-te pli-ro-fo-rí-es yia to-pi-ká fes-ti-vál?)

181. Is there Wi-Fi available on long bus journeys?
Υπάρχει Wi-Fi σε μακρινά ταξίδια με λεωφορείο;
(I-pár-hi Wi-Fi se mak-ri-ná tak-sí-di-a me le-o-fo-reí-o?)

> **Fun Fact:** The frappe, a foam-covered iced coffee drink,
> was invented in Greece in 1957.

182. Where can I rent a bicycle for exploring the city?
Πού μπορώ να νοικιάσω ποδήλατο για να εξερευνήσω την
πόλη;
*(Poú bo-ró na ni-kiá-so po-dí-la-to yia na ek-se-rev-ní-so tin
pó-li?)*

> **Travel Story:** On a ferry to Mykonos, a sailor said, "Η
> θάλασσα δεν έχει βασιλιά," meaning "The sea has no
> king," reflecting the unpredictability of the ocean.

Getting Around by Public Transportation

183. Which bus should I take to reach the city center?
Ποιο λεωφορείο πρέπει να πάρω για να φτάσω στο κέντρο της πόλης;
(Pee-o le-o-fo-reí-o pré-pi na pá-ro yia na ftá-so sto kén-tro tis pó-lis?)

184. Can I buy a day pass for unlimited rides?
Μπορώ να αγοράσω ημερήσια κάρτα για απεριόριστες διαδρομές;
(Bo-ró na a-go-rá-so i-me-rí-sia kár-ta yia a-pe-rió-ri-stes di-a-dro-més?)

185. Is there a metro station within walking distance?
Υπάρχει σταθμός μετρό σε απόσταση πεζοπορίας;
(I-pár-hi sta-thmós me-tró se a-pós-ta-si pe-zo-po-rí-as?)

186. How do I transfer between different bus lines?
Πώς μεταβαίνω από τη μία σε άλλη λεωφορειακή γραμμή;
(Pós me-ta-ve-í-no a-pó ti mí-a se ál-li le-o-fo-rei-a-kí gram-mí?)

187. Are there any discounts for senior citizens?
Υπάρχουν έκπτωσεις για ηλικιωμένους;
(I-pár-houn ék-p-to-seis yia i-li-ki-o-mé-nous?)

188. What's the last bus/train for the night?
Ποιο είναι το τελευταίο λεωφορείο/τρένο για το βράδυ;
(Pee-o ee-ne to te-lef-té-o le-o-fo-reí-o/tré-no yia to vrá-di?)

189. Are there any express buses to [destination]?
Υπάρχουν εκφρεσικά λεωφορεία προς [προορισμό];
(I-pár-houn ek-fre-si-ká le-o-fo-reí-a pros [pro-o-ris-mó]?)

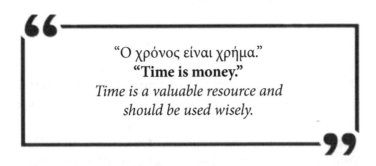

"Ο χρόνος είναι χρήμα."
"Time is money."
*Time is a valuable resource and
should be used wisely.*

190. Do trams run on weekends as well?
Τραμ λειτουργούν και τα σαββατοκύριακα;
(Tram lei-tour-goún ke ta sav-va-to-kí-ri-a-ka?)

> **Fun Fact:** Souvlaki is a popular Greek fast food consisting of small pieces of meat and sometimes vegetables grilled on a skewer.

191. Can you recommend a reliable taxi service?
Μπορείτε να προτείνετε ένα αξιόπιστο ταξί;
(Bo-ree-te na pro-tí-ne-te é-na a-xió-pis-to tak-sí?)

192. What's the fare for a one-way ticket to the suburbs?
Πόσο κοστίζει ένα εισιτήριο μονής διαδρομής για τα προάστια;
(Pó-so kos-tí-zei é-na ei-si-tí-rio mo-nís di-a-dro-mís yia ta pro-ás-tia?)

> **Travel Story:** In a traditional taverna in Nafplio, the owner described his secret recipe as "Αλά κρητικά," meaning "Cretan style," famous for its unique flavors.

Navigating the Airport

193. Where can I locate the baggage claim area?
Πού μπορώ να βρω την περιοχή παραλαβής αποσκευών;
(Poú bo-ró na vró tin pe-ri-o-hí pa-ra-la-vís a-po-ske-vón?)

194. Is there a currency exchange counter in the terminal?
Υπάρχει γραφείο συναλλαγματικής ανταλλαγής στο τερματικό;
(I-pár-hi gra-fí-o si-nal-la-gma-ti-kís an-tal-la-gís sto ter-ma-ti-kó?)

> **Idiomatic Expression:** "Σε βλέπω στα γρήγορα." - Meaning: "See you soon."
> (Literal translation: "I see you quickly.")

195. Are there any pet relief areas for service animals?
Υπάρχουν χώροι αναψυχής για τα ζώα συνοδείας;
(I-pár-houn hó-roi a-na-psy-hís yia ta zóa si-no-dí-as?)

196. How early can I go through security?
Πόσο νωρίς μπορώ να περάσω τον έλεγχο ασφαλείας;
(Pó-so no-rís bo-ró na pe-rá-so ton é-len-ho as-fa-leí-as?)

197. What's the procedure for boarding the aircraft?
Ποια είναι η διαδικασία επιβίβασης στο αεροπλάνο;
(Pee-a ee-ne ee di-a-di-ka-sí-a e-pi-ví-va-sis sto ae-ro-plá-no?)

198. Can I use mobile boarding passes?
Μπορώ να χρησιμοποιήσω κινητές κάρτες επιβίβασης;
(Bo-ró na hri-si-mo-poi-í-so ki-ni-tés kár-tes e-pi-ví-va-sis?)

199. Are there any restaurants past security?
Υπάρχουν εστιατόρια μετά τον έλεγχο ασφαλείας;
(I-pár-houn es-ti-a-tó-ria me-tá ton é-len-ho as-fa-leí-as?)

200. What's the airport's Wi-Fi password?
Ποιος είναι ο κωδικός Wi-Fi του αεροδρομίου;
(Pee-os ee-ne o ko-di-kós Wi-Fi tou ae-ro-dro-mí-ou?)

201. Can I bring duty-free items on board?
Μπορώ να φέρω αφορολόγητα είδη μαζί μου στο αεροπλάνο;
(Bo-ró na fé-ro a-fo-ro-ló-gi-ta eí-di ma-zí mou sto ae-ro-plá-no?)

202. Is there a pharmacy at the airport?
Υπάρχει φαρμακείο στο αεροδρόμιο;
(I-pár-hi far-ma-keí-o sto ae-ro-dró-mio?)

Traveling by Car

203. How do I pay tolls on the highway?
Πώς πληρώνω τα διόδια στον αυτοκινητόδρομο;
(Pós pli-ró-no ta di-ó-di-a ston af-to-ki-ni-tó-dro-mo?)

204. Where can I find a car wash nearby?
Πού μπορώ να βρω κοντινό αυτοκινητοπλυντήριο;
(Poú bo-ró na vró kon-ti-nó af-to-ki-ni-to-plyn-tí-rio?)

205. Are there electric vehicle charging stations?
Υπάρχουν σταθμοί φόρτισης για ηλεκτρικά αυτοκίνητα;
(I-pár-houn sta-thmí fór-ti-sis yia i-lek-tri-ká af-to-kí-ni-ta?)

206.   Can I rent a GPS navigation system with the car?
       Μπορώ να νοικιάσω σύστημα πλοήγησης GPS με το
       αυτοκίνητο;
       (Bo-ró na ni-kiá-so sí-sti-ma plo-í-gi-sis GPS me to
       af-to-kí-ni-to?)

207.   What's the cost of parking in the city center?
       Πόσο κοστίζει το παρκάρισμα στο κέντρο της πόλης;
       (Pó-so kos-tí-zei to par-ká-ri-sma sto kén-tro tis pó-lis?)

208.   Do I need an international driving permit?
       Χρειάζομαι διεθνή άδεια οδήγησης;
       (Hre-iá-zo-mai di-e-thní á-de-ia o-dí-gi-sis?)

209.   Is roadside assistance available?
       Υπάρχει οδική βοήθεια;
       (I-pár-hi o-di-kí vo-í-thei-a?)

210.   Are there any traffic cameras on this route?
       Υπάρχουν κάμερες κυκλοφορίας σε αυτή τη διαδρομή;
       (I-pár-houn ká-me-res ky-klo-fo-rí-as se af-tí ti di-a-dro-mí?)

211.   Can you recommend a reliable mechanic?
       Μπορείτε να προτείνετε έναν αξιόπιστο μηχανικό;
       (Bo-ree-te na pro-tí-ne-te é-nan a-xió-pis-to mi-ha-ni-kó?)

212.   What's the speed limit in residential areas?
       Ποιο είναι το όριο ταχύτητας στις κατοικημένες περιοχές;
       (Pee-o ee-ne to ó-rio ta-hí-ti-tas stis ka-toi-ki-mé-nes pe-ri-o-hés?)

Airport Transfers and Shuttles

213. Where is the taxi stand located at the airport?
Πού βρίσκεται η στάση ταξί στο αεροδρόμιο;
(Poú vrís-ke-tai ee stá-si tak-sí sto ae-ro-dró-mio?)

214. Do airport shuttles run 24/7?
Λειτουργούν τα λεωφορεία του αεροδρομίου 24 ώρες το 24ωρο;
(Lei-tour-goún ta le-o-fo-reí-a tou ae-ro-dro-mí-ou éf-di kát-i katá éf-di?)

> Idiomatic Expression: "Σκάω σαν ποπ κορν." - Meaning: "I'm bursting with excitement or anger." (Literal translation: "I burst like popcorn.")

215. How long does it take to reach downtown by taxi?
Πόσο χρόνο χρειάζεται για να φτάσω στο κέντρο με ταξί;
(Pó-so hró-no hre-iá-ze-tai yia na ftá-so sto kén-tro me tak-sí?)

216. Is there a designated pick-up area for ride-sharing services?
Υπάρχει ορισμένη περιοχή για την επιβίβαση υπηρεσιών κοινόχρηστης μετακίνησης;
(I-pár-hi o-ri-sme-ní pe-ri-o-hí yia tin e-pi-ví-va-si i-pe-re-sión ki-nó-hri-stis me-ta-kí-ni-sis?)

217. Can I book a shuttle in advance?
Μπορώ να κάνω κράτηση για λεωφορείο μεταφοράς εκ των προτέρων;
(Bo-ró na ká-no krá-ti-si yia le-o-fo-reí-o me-ta-fó-ras ek ton pro-té-ron?)

> Fun Fact: Tzatziki, a famous Greek sauce, is made from yogurt, garlic, and cucumber.

218.   Do hotels offer free shuttle service to the airport?
       Προσφέρουν τα ξενοδοχεία δωρεάν μεταφορά στο
       αεροδρόμιο;
       (Pro-sfé-roun ta kse-no-do-hí-a do-ré-an me-ta-fo-rá sto
       ae-ro-dró-mio?)

219.   What's the rate for a private airport transfer?
       Πόσο κοστίζει μια ιδιωτική μεταφορά στο αεροδρόμιο;
       (Pó-so kos-tí-zei mi-a i-di-o-ti-kí me-ta-fo-rá sto ae-ro-dró-mio?)

220.   Are there any public buses connecting to the airport?
       Υπάρχουν δημόσια λεωφορεία που συνδέουν με το
       αεροδρόμιο;
       (I-pár-houn di-mó-sia le-o-fo-reí-a pou sin-dé-oun me to
       ae-ro-dró-mio?)

221.   Can you recommend a reliable limousine service?
       Μπορείτε να προτείνετε μια αξιόπιστη λιμουζίνα;
       (Bo-ree-te na pro-tí-ne-te mi-a a-xió-pis-ti li-mou-zí-na?)

222.   Is there an airport shuttle for early morning flights?
       Υπάρχει λεωφορείο για το αεροδρόμιο για τις πρωινές
       πτήσεις;
       (I-pár-hi le-o-fo-reí-o yia to ae-ro-dró-mio yia tis pro-i-nés
       ptí-seis?)

Traveling with Luggage

223.   Can I check my bags at this train station?
       Μπορώ να ελέγξω τις αποσκευές μου σε αυτόν τον σταθμό;
       (Bo-ró na e-lé-xo tis a-po-ske-vés mou se af-tón ton sta-thmó?)

224. Where can I find baggage carts in the airport?
Πού μπορώ να βρω καροτσάκια για αποσκευές στο
αεροδρόμιο;
*(Poú bo-ró na vró ka-rot-sá-kia yia a-po-ske-vés sto
ae-ro-dró-mio?)*

> **Fun Fact:** In ancient Olympic Games, athletes competed
> nude to celebrate the human body.

225. Are there weight limits for checked baggage?
Υπάρχουν όρια βάρους για τις ελεγχόμενες αποσκευές;
(I-pár-houn ó-ria vá-rous yia tis e-len-hó-me-nes a-po-ske-vés?)

226. Can I carry my backpack as a personal item?
Μπορώ να πάρω το σακίδιο μου ως προσωπικό αντικείμενο;
*(Bo-ró na pá-ro to sa-kí-dio mou os pro-so-pi-kó
an-ti-kéi-me-no?)*

227. What's the procedure for oversized luggage?
Ποια είναι η διαδικασία για τις υπερμεγέθη αποσκευές;
*(Pee-a ee-ne ee di-a-di-ka-sí-a yia tis i-pe-rme-gé-thi
a-po-ske-vés?)*

228. Can I bring a stroller on the bus?
Μπορώ να φέρω το καροτσάκι στο λεωφορείο;
(Bo-ró na fé-ro to ka-rot-sá-ki sto le-o-fo-reí-o?)

229. Are there lockers for storing luggage at the airport?
Υπάρχουν ντουλάπια για τη φύλαξη αποσκευών στο
αεροδρόμιο;
*(I-pár-houn ndou-lá-pia yia ti fí-la-xi a-po-ske-vón sto
ae-ro-dró-mio?)*

> **Fun Fact:** Greek mythology has profoundly influenced
> Western culture, art, and literature.

230.   How do I label my luggage with contact information?
Πώς μπορώ να επισημάνω τις αποσκευές μου με πληροφορίες επικοινωνίας;
(Pós bo-ró na e-pi-si-má-no tis a-po-ske-vés mou me pli-ro-fo-rí-es e-pi-ko-i-no-ní-as?)

231.   Is there a lost and found office at the train station?
Υπάρχει γραφείο αντικειμένων που βρέθηκαν στο σταθμό του τρένου;
(I-pár-hi gra-fí-o an-ti-kei-mé-non pou vré-thi-kan sto sta-thmó tou tré-nou?)

> **Idiomatic Expression:** "Μπαίνω στο χορό." -
> Meaning: "Join in."
> (Literal translation: "I enter the dance.")

232.   Can I carry fragile items in my checked bags?
Μπορώ να μεταφέρω ευαίσθητα αντικείμενα στις ελεγχόμενες αποσκευές μου;
(Bo-ró na me-ta-fé-ro e-vé-s-the-ta an-ti-keí-me-na stis e-len-hó-me-nes a-po-ske-vés mou?)

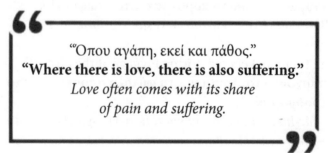

"Όπου αγάπη, εκεί και πάθος."
"Where there is love, there is also suffering."
Love often comes with its share of pain and suffering.

Word Search Puzzle: Travel & Transportation

AIRPORT
ΑΕΡΟΔΡΌΜΙΟ
BUS
ΛΕΩΦΟΡΕΊΟ
TAXI
ΤΑΞΙ
TICKET
ΕΙΣΙΤΉΡΙΟ
MAP
ΧΆΡΤΗΣ
CAR
ΑΥΤΟΚΊΝΗΤΟ
METRO
ΜΕΤΡΌ
BICYCLE
ΠΟΔΉΛΑΤΟ
DEPARTURE
ΑΝΑΧΏΡΗΣΗ
ARRIVAL
ΆΦΙΞΗ
ROAD
ΔΡΌΜΟΣ
PLATFORM
ΠΛΑΤΦΌΡΜΑ
STATION
ΣΤΑΘΜΌΣ
TERMINAL
ΤΕΡΜΑΤΙΚΌΣ

```
L  Ί  B  H  F  E  Y  V  K  I  G  G  W  P  J
P  I  Ξ  A  A  L  H  P  T  G  X  Q  P  N  B
A  M  F  A  P  C  D  A  O  R  X  M  A  Q  J
R  E  D  R  T  Y  D  E  P  A  R  T  U  R  E
R  S  C  W  C  C  S  T  A  T  I  O  N  N  T
I  E  M  M  Z  I  T  W  N  D  L  Z  U  W  A
V  Z  T  R  G  B  V  L  V  S  I  T  G  Y  Α
A  F  E  O  V  A  I  R  P  O  R  T  T  Φ  A
L  E  K  F  A  U  Σ  T  L  U  Q  O  I  M  C
F  H  C  T  S  N  D  O  R  L  K  Ξ  P  S  Λ
A  N  I  A  Σ  C  A  Z  M  Ί  H  Ό  H  E  F
O  E  T  L  I  T  N  X  N  Ό  Φ  J  Ω  N  R
D  K  P  P  M  U  A  H  Ω  T  P  Φ  G  U  P
Z  Y  U  O  R  Z  T  Θ  A  P  O  Δ  K  N  N
Z  Z  V  V  Δ  O  F  Λ  M  P  H  F  P  O  H
M  L  A  S  O  P  Π  F  E  Ό  S  Σ  A  I  O
Z  V  E  S  H  T  Ό  Ί  M  A  Σ  K  H  I  O
N  D  Z  K  T  X  O  M  I  X  A  T  P  T  T
X  W  K  C  X  N  B  N  I  J  F  Ή  A  S  E
Z  Α  N  X  E  H  U  I  W  O  T  Λ  H  T  R
G  W  P  G  K  Q  S  A  H  I  Ή  Q  E  Z  M
L  W  J  T  D  G  B  N  Σ  Δ  V  P  Z  O  I
M  I  E  C  H  U  M  I  O  J  M  V  T  J  N
A  C  T  A  Ό  Σ  E  Π  S  A  T  B  B  N  A
S  Y  V  R  A  P  T  X  T  A  B  K  H  D  L
O  J  E  T  O  T  T  I  E  Z  J  N  U  O  S
O  R  T  E  M  Y  K  E  T  G  T  V  R  X  C
O  H  M  X  H  Ό  Q  F  M  Z  P  F  K  J  C
I  L  C  Z  Σ  M  E  B  P  Q  S  R  T  Y  P
D  L  B  B  G  N  S  W  B  H  P  M  A  P  D
```

59

Correct Answers:

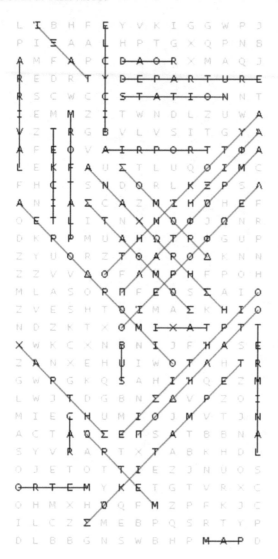

ACCOMMODATIONS

- CHECKING INTO A HOTEL -
- ASKING ABOUT ROOM AMENITIES -
- REPORTING ISSUES OR MAKING REQUESTS -

Hotel Check-In

233. I have a reservation under [Name].
   Έχω κράτηση στο όνομα [Όνομα].
   (É-ho krá-ti-si sto ó-no-ma [Ó-no-ma].)

234. Can I see some identification, please?
   Μπορώ να δω κάποιο ταυτοτικό έγγραφο, παρακαλώ;
   (Bo-ró na do ká-pio taf-to-ti-kó én-gra-fo, pa-ra-ka-ló?)

235. What time is check-in/check-out?
   Ποια ώρα είναι το check-in/check-out;
   (Pee-a ó-ra ee-ne to check-in/check-out?)

236. Is breakfast included in the room rate?
   Συμπεριλαμβάνεται το πρωινό στην τιμή του δωματίου;
   (Sim-pe-ri-lam-vá-ne-tai to pro-i-nó stin ti-mí tou do-ma-tí-ou?)

237. Do you need a credit card for incidentals?
   Χρειάζεται πιστωτική κάρτα για πρόσθετες χρεώσεις;
   (Hre-iá-ze-tai pis-to-ti-kí kár-ta yia prós-the-tes hre-ó-seis?)

238. May I have a room key, please?
   Μπορώ να έχω το κλειδί του δωματίου, παρακαλώ;
   (Bo-ró na é-ho to kli-di tou do-ma-tí-ou, pa-ra-ka-ló?)

239. Is there a shuttle service to the airport?
   Υπάρχει υπηρεσία shuttle για το αεροδρόμιο;
   (I-pár-hi i-pe-re-sí-a shuttle yia to ae-ro-dró-mio?)

240.   Could you call a bellhop for assistance?
       Μπορείτε να καλέσετε έναν υπάλληλο για βοήθεια;
       (*Bo-ree-te na ka-lé-se-te é-nan i-pá-li-lo yia vo-í-thei-a?*)

> **Fun Fact:** The admiration for Greek culture, language, and history is known as philhellenism.

Room Amenities

241.   Can I request a non-smoking room?
       Μπορώ να ζητήσω δωμάτιο για μη καπνιστές;
       (*Bo-ró na zi-tí-so do-má-tio yia mi kap-ni-stés?*)

242.   Is there a mini-fridge in the room?
       Υπάρχει μίνι ψυγείο στο δωμάτιο;
       (*I-pár-hi mí-ni p-si-yí-o sto do-má-tio?*)

243.   Do you provide free Wi-Fi access?
       Παρέχετε δωρεάν πρόσβαση στο Wi-Fi;
       (*Pa-ré-hete do-ré-an pró-sva-si sto Wi-Fi?*)

244.   Can I have an extra pillow or blanket?
       Μπορώ να έχω ένα επιπλέον μαξιλάρι ή κουβέρτα;
       (*Bo-ró na é-ho é-na e-pi-plé-on ma-xi-lá-ri í kou-vér-ta?*)

245.   Is there a hairdryer in the bathroom?
       Υπάρχει στεγνωτήρας μαλλιών στο μπάνιο;
       (*I-pár-hi ste-gno-tí-ras ma-li-ón sto bá-nio?*)

246. What's the TV channel lineup?
Ποια είναι τα τηλεοπτικά κανάλια;
(Pee-a ee-ne ta ti-le-op-ti-ká ka-ná-lia?)

247. Are toiletries like shampoo provided?
Παρέχονται τουαλέτες όπως σαμπουάν;
(Pa-ré-hon-te tou-a-lé-tes ó-pos sam-pou-án?)

248. Is room service available 24/7?
Υπάρχει διαθέσιμη υπηρεσία δωματίου 24 ώρες την ημέρα;
(I-pár-hi di-a-thé-si-mi i-pe-re-sí-a do-ma-tí-ou éf-di ó-res tin i-mé-ra?)

> Fun Fact: Greece has the most archaeological museums in the world.

Reporting Issues

249. There's a problem with the air conditioning.
Υπάρχει πρόβλημα με τον κλιματισμό.
(I-pár-hi pró-vli-ma me ton kli-ma-tis-mó.)

250. The shower is not working properly.
Το ντους δεν λειτουργεί σωστά.
(To dous den lei-tour-ghí so-stá.)

251. My room key card isn't functioning.
Η κάρτα του δωματίου μου δεν λειτουργεί.
(Ee kár-ta tou do-ma-tí-ou mou den lei-tour-ghí.)

252. There's a leak in the bathroom.
Υπάρχει διαρροή στο μπάνιο.
(*I-pár-hi di-ar-ró-i sto bá-nio.*)

253. The TV remote is not responding.
Το τηλεκοντρόλ της τηλεόρασης δεν ανταποκρίνεται.
(*To ti-le-kon-tról tis ti-le-ó-ra-sis den an-ta-po-krí-ne-tai.*)

254. Can you fix the broken light in my room?
Μπορείτε να επισκευάσετε το χαλασμένο φως στο δωμάτιό μου;
(*Bo-ree-te na e-pi-ske-vá-se-te to ha-las-mé-no fos sto do-má-tio mou?*)

255. I need assistance with my luggage.
Χρειάζομαι βοήθεια με τις αποσκευές μου.
(*Hre-iá-zo-mai vo-í-thei-a me tis a-po-ske-vés mou.*)

256. There's a strange noise coming from next door.
Ακούγεται ένας περίεργος θόρυβος από το διπλανό δωμάτιο.
(*A-koú-ge-tai é-nas pe-rí-er-gos thó-ry-vos a-pó to di-pla-nó do-má-tio.*)

Making Requests

257. Can I have a wake-up call at 7 AM?
Μπορώ να έχω ένα ξυπνητήρι στις 7 το πρωί;
(*Bo-ró na é-ho é-na xi-pni-tí-ri stis ef-tá to pro-í?*)

Fun Fact: Greece is home to historical sites like the Acropolis, Delphi, and Medieval City of Rhodes.

258. Please send extra towels to my room.
Παρακαλώ, στείλτε επιπλέον πετσέτες στο δωμάτιό μου.
(*Pa-ra-ka-ló, stíl-te e-pi-plé-on pe-tsé-tes sto do-má-tio mou.*)

259. Could you arrange a taxi for tomorrow?
Μπορείτε να κανονίσετε ένα ταξί για αύριο;
(*Bo-ree-te na ka-no-ní-se-te é-na tak-sí yia á-vrio?*)

260. I'd like to extend my stay for two more nights.
Θα ήθελα να παρατείνω τη διαμονή μου για άλλες δύο νύχτες
(*Tha í-the-la na pa-ra-tí-no ti dia-mo-ní mou yia ál-les dýo níh-tes.*)

> **Idiomatic Expression:** "Ο,τι λαχεί!" -
> Meaning: "Whatever happens!"
> (Literal translation: "Whatever is drawn!")

261. Is it possible to change my room?
Είναι δυνατόν να αλλάξω το δωμάτιό μου;
(*Eí-nai dy-na-tón na al-lá-xo to do-má-tio mou?*)

262. Can I have a late check-out at 2 PM?
Μπορώ να έχω αργό check-out στις 2 το μεσημέρι;
(*Bo-ró na é-ho ar-gó check-out stis dýo to me-si-mé-ri?*)

263. I need an iron and ironing board.
Χρειάζομαι σίδερο και σιδερώστρα.
(*Hre-iá-zo-mai sí-de-ro kai si-de-rós-tra.*)

264. Could you provide directions to [location]?
Μπορείτε να μου δώσετε οδηγίες για [τοποθεσία];
(*Bo-ree-te na mou dó-se-te o-di-gí-es yia [to-po-the-sí-a]?*)

Room Types and Preferences

265. I'd like to book a single room, please.
Θα ήθελα να κλείσω μία μονόκλινη δωμάτιο, παρακαλώ.
(*Tha í-the-la na klí-so mí-a mo-nó-kli-ni do-má-tio, pa-ra-ka-ló.*)

266. Do you have any suites available?
Έχετε διαθέσιμες σουίτες;
(*É-he-te di-a-thé-si-mes sou-í-tes?*)

267. Is there a room with a view of the city?
Υπάρχει δωμάτιο με θέα στην πόλη;
(*I-pár-hi do-má-tio me thé-a stin pó-li?*)

268. Is breakfast included in the room rate?
Συμπεριλαμβάνεται το πρωινό στην τιμή του δωματίου;
(*Sim-pe-ri-lam-vá-ne-tai to pro-i-nó stin ti-mí tou do-ma-tí-ou?*)

269. Can I request a room on a higher floor?
Μπορώ να ζητήσω δωμάτιο σε υψηλότερο όροφο;
(*Bo-ró na zi-tí-so do-má-tio se i-psi-ló-te-ro ó-ro-fo?*)

270. Is there an option for a smoking room?
Υπάρχει επιλογή για δωμάτιο καπνιζόντων;
(*I-pár-hi e-pi-lo-gí yia do-má-tio kap-ni-zón-don?*)

> **Travel Story:** At a monastery in Meteora, a monk said,
> "Το νερό τρέχει, αλλά οι πέτρες μένουν," meaning
> "Water flows, but the stones remain," signifying the
> endurance of faith.

271. Are there connecting rooms for families?
Υπάρχουν ενωμένα δωμάτια για οικογένειες;
(*I-pár-houn e-no-mé-na do-má-tia yia i-ko-gé-ni-es?*)

272. I'd prefer a king-size bed.
Θα προτιμούσα ένα κρεβάτι king-size.
(*Tha pro-ti-móu-sa é-na kre-vá-ti king-size.*)

273. Is there a bathtub in any of the rooms?
Υπάρχει μπανιέρα σε κάποια από τα δωμάτια;
(*I-pár-hi ba-nié-ra se ká-pi-a a-pó ta do-má-tia?*)

Hotel Facilities and Services

274. What time does the hotel restaurant close?
Πότε κλείνει το εστιατόριο του ξενοδοχείου;
(*Pó-te kleí-nei to es-ti-a-tó-rio tou kse-no-do-hí-ou?*)

275. Is there a fitness center in the hotel?
Υπάρχει γυμναστήριο στο ξενοδοχείο;
(*I-pár-hi gym-nas-tí-rio sto kse-no-do-hí-o?*)

276. Can I access the pool as a guest?
Μπορώ ως επισκέπτης να χρησιμοποιήσω την πισίνα;
(*Bo-ró os e-pi-skép-tis na hri-si-mo-poi-í-so tin pi-sí-na?*)

277. Do you offer laundry facilities?
Προσφέρετε υπηρεσίες πλυντηρίου;
(*Pro-sfé-re-te i-pe-re-sí-es plin-ti-ri-ou?*)

278. Is parking available on-site?
Υπάρχει διαθέσιμο πάρκινγκ στον χώρο του ξενοδοχείου;
(I-pár-hi di-a-thé-si-mo pá-rkin-gk ston hó-ro tou kse-no-do-hí-ou?)

279. Is room cleaning provided daily?
Παρέχεται καθημερινή καθαριότητα στα δωμάτια;
(Pa-ré-he-tai ka-thi-me-ri-ní ka-tha-rió-ti-ta sta do-má-tia?)

280. Can I use the business center?
Μπορώ να χρησιμοποιήσω το κέντρο επιχειρήσεων;
(Bo-ró na hri-si-mo-poi-í-so to kén-tro e-pi-hei-rí-se-on?)

281. Are pets allowed in the hotel?
Επιτρέπονται κατοικίδια στο ξενοδοχείο;
(E-pi-tré-pon-tai ka-toi-kí-di-a sto kse-no-do-hí-o?)

> **Travel Story:** In Rhodes, a historian referred to the ancient walls as "Μάρτυρες του χρόνου," meaning "Witnesses of time," symbolizing their historical significance.

Payment and Check-Out

282. Can I have the bill, please?
Μπορώ να έχω τον λογαριασμό, παρακαλώ;
(Bo-ró na é-ho ton lo-ga-ri-as-mó, pa-ra-ka-ló?)

283. Do you accept credit cards?
Δέχεστε πιστωτικές κάρτες;
(Dé-he-ste pis-to-ti-kés kár-tes?)

284. Can I pay in cash?
Μπορώ να πληρώσω με μετρητά;
(Bo-ró na pli-ró-so me me-tri-tá?)

285. Is there a security deposit required?
Απαιτείται κατάθεση εγγύησης;
(A-pe-té-i-tai ka-tá-the-si eg-gí-i-sis?)

286. Can I get a receipt for my stay?
Μπορώ να πάρω απόδειξη για τη διαμονή μου;
(Bo-ró na pá-ro a-pó-di-xi yia ti dia-mo-ní mou?)

287. What's the check-out time?
Ποια είναι η ώρα αναχώρησης;
(Pee-a ee-ne i ó-ra a-na-hó-ri-sis?)

288. Is late check-out an option?
Υπάρχει επιλογή για αργή αναχώρηση;
(I-pár-hi e-pi-lo-gí yia ar-gí a-na-hó-ri-si?)

289. Can I settle my bill in advance?
Μπορώ να εξοφλήσω το λογαριασμό μου εκ των προτέρων;
(Bo-ró na ek-so-flí-so to lo-ga-ri-as-mó mou ek ton pro-té-ron?)

Booking Accommodations

290. Can I book online or by phone?
Μπορώ να κάνω κράτηση διαδικτυακά ή τηλεφωνικά;
(Bo-ró na ká-no krá-ti-si dia-dik-tia-ká í ti-le-fo-ni-ká?)

291. How much is the room rate per night?
Πόσο κοστίζει η δωμάτιο ανά νύχτα;
(*Pó-so kos-tí-zei i do-má-tio a-ná níh-ta?*)

292. I'd like to make a reservation.
Θα ήθελα να κάνω μια κράτηση.
(*Tha í-the-la na ká-no mi-a krá-ti-si.*)

293. Are there any special promotions?
Υπάρχουν κάποιες ειδικές προσφορές;
(*I-pár-houn ká-pi-es i-di-kés pro-sfo-rés?*)

294. Is breakfast included in the booking?
Συμπεριλαμβάνεται το πρωινό στην κράτηση;
(*Sim-pe-ri-lam-vá-ne-tai to pro-i-nó stin krá-ti-si?*)

295. Can you confirm my reservation?
Μπορείτε να επιβεβαιώσετε την κράτησή μου;
(*Bo-ree-te na e-pi-ve-ve-aó-se-te tin krá-ti-sí mou?*)

296. What's the cancellation policy?
Ποια είναι η πολιτική ακύρωσης;
(*Pee-a ee-ne i po-li-ti-kí a-kí-ro-sis?*)

297. I'd like to modify my booking.
Θα ήθελα να τροποποιήσω την κράτησή μου.
(*Tha í-the-la na tro-po-po-ií-so tin krá-ti-sí mou.*)

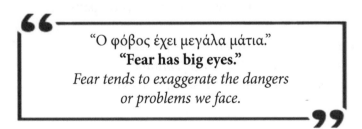

"Ο φόβος έχει μεγάλα μάτια."
"Fear has big eyes."
*Fear tends to exaggerate the dangers
or problems we face.*

Mini Lesson:
Basic Grammar Principles in Greek #1

Introduction:

Greek, an ancient language with a rich history and significant influence on Western culture and language, continues to be spoken in Greece and parts of Cyprus. Greek's unique alphabet and complex grammar structure present a fascinating challenge for learners. This lesson covers fundamental grammar concepts necessary for beginners embarking on their Greek language journey.

1. Alphabet and Pronunciation:

Greek uses the Greek alphabet, consisting of 24 letters. Each letter has a unique sound, and pronunciation is phonetic:

- *A, α (Alpha) - sounds like 'a' in "father"*
- *B, β (Beta) - sounds like 'v' in "victory"*
- *Γ, γ (Gamma) - sounds like 'y' in "yellow" before E, I, and like 'g' in "good" before A, O, Y*

2. Nouns and Gender:

Greek nouns are divided into three genders: masculine, feminine, and neuter. Each gender has its own set of declension patterns:

- *o φίλος (o fílos - the friend) - masculine*
- *η μέρα (i méra - the day) - feminine*
- *το βιβλίο (to vivlío - the book) - neuter*

3. Articles:

Greek has definite and indefinite articles, which agree in gender, number, and case with the noun they modify:

- *o, η, το (o, i, to - the) - definite articles*
- *ένας, μία, ένα (énas, mía, éna - a/an) - indefinite articles*

4. Verb Conjugation:

Greek verbs are conjugated based on tense, mood, voice, person, and number. Verbs change forms to align with their subject:

- *Μιλάω (miláo - I speak)*
- *Έλεγε (élege - he/she/it was saying)*

5. Tenses:

Greek has several tenses to express time aspects, including present, past, and future. Each tense has its own conjugation pattern:

- *Πηγαίνω (pigéno - I go/I am going - present)*
- *Πήγα (píga - I went - past simple)*
- *Θα πάω (tha páo - I will go - future)*

6. Adjectives:

Adjectives in Greek agree with the noun they modify in gender, number, and case:

- *έξυπνος φίλος (éxipnos fílos - smart friend) - masculine*
- *έξυπνη φίλη (éxipni fíli - smart friend) - feminine*

7. Prepositions:

Prepositions in Greek are used to express relations of nouns or pronouns to the rest of the sentence and often require nouns to be in a specific case:

- *Στο σπίτι (sto spíti - in the house)*
- *Με τον φίλο (me ton fílo - with the friend)*

Conclusion:

This introductory overview of Greek grammar lays the groundwork for further exploration and study. Greek grammar's intricacies and nuances become more manageable with practice. Keep engaging with Greek media and conversation for more profound learning. Καλή τύχη! (Good luck!)

SHOPPING

- BARGAINING AND HAGGLING -
- DESCRIBING ITEMS AND SIZES -
- MAKING PURCHASES AND PAYMENTS -

Bargaining

298.   Can you give me a discount?
       Μπορείτε να μου κάνετε έκπτωση;
       (Bo-ree-te na mou ká-ne-te ék-p-to-si?)

299.   What's your best price?
       Ποια είναι η καλύτερη τιμή σας;
       (Pee-a ee-ne i ka-lí-te-ri ti-mí sas?)

300.   Is this the final price?
       Αυτή είναι η τελική τιμή;
       (Af-tí ee-ne i te-li-kí ti-mí?)

301.   What's the lowest you can go?
       Ποια είναι η χαμηλότερη τιμή που μπορείτε να προσφέρετε;
       (Pee-a ee-ne i ha-mi-ló-te-ri ti-mí pou bo-ree-te na pro-sfé-re-te?)

302.   Do you offer any discounts for cash payments?
       Προσφέρετε κάποια έκπτωση για πληρωμές με μετρητά;
       (Pro-sfé-re-te ká-pi-a ék-p-to-si yia pli-ro-més me me-tri-tá?)

303.   Are there any promotions or deals?
       Υπάρχουν κάποιες προσφορές ή ειδικές προωθήσεις;
       (I-pár-houn ká-pi-es pro-sfo-rés í i-di-kés pro-o-thí-seis?)

304.   I'm on a budget. Can you lower the price?
       Έχω περιορισμένο budget. Μπορείτε να μειώσετε την τιμή;
       (É-ho pe-ri-o-ris-mé-no budget. Bo-ree-te na mió-se-te tin ti-mí?)

305. I'd like to negotiate the price.
Θα ήθελα να διαπραγματευτώ την τιμή.
(Tha í-the-la na di-a-prag-ma-tef-tó tin ti-mí.)

306. Can you do any better on the price?
Μπορείτε να κάνετε καλύτερη προσφορά στην τιμή;
(Bo-ree-te na ká-ne-te ka-lí-te-ri pro-sfo-rá stin ti-mí?)

307. Can you match the price from your competitor?
Μπορείτε να ταιριάξετε την τιμή του ανταγωνιστή σας;
(Bo-ree-te na te-riá-xe-te tin ti-mí tou an-ta-go-nis-tí sas?)

Item Descriptions

308. Can you tell me about this product?
Μπορείτε να μου πείτε για αυτό το προϊόν;
(Bo-ree-te na mou peí-te yia af-tó to pro-í-on?)

309. What are the specifications of this item?
Ποιες είναι οι προδιαγραφές αυτού του προϊόντος;
(Pee-es ee-ne i pro-di-a-gra-fés af-tú tou pro-í-on-tos?)

310. Is this available in different colors?
Υπάρχει διαθέσιμο σε διαφορετικά χρώματα;
(I-pár-hi di-a-thé-si-mo se dia-fo-re-ti-ká hro-ma-ta?)

311. Can you explain how this works?
Μπορείτε να μου εξηγήσετε πώς λειτουργεί αυτό;
(Bo-ree-te na mou ex-i-gí-se-te pós lei-tour-gí af-tó?)

312. What's the material of this item?
Από τι υλικό είναι φτιαγμένο αυτό το προϊόν;
(Apó ti yli-kó í-ne fti-agmé-no af-tó to pro-í-on?)

313. Are there any warranties or guarantees?
Υπάρχουν εγγυήσεις ή εγγύηση για αυτό το προϊόν;
(I-pár-houn eg-gí-i-sis í eg-gí-i-si yia af-tó to pro-í-on?)

314. Does it come with accessories?
Συνοδεύεται με αξεσουάρ;
(Si-no-dé-ve-tai me ak-se-sou-ár?)

315. Can you show me how to use this?
Μπορείτε να μου δείξετε πώς χρησιμοποιείται αυτό;
(Bo-ree-te na mou dí-xe-te pós hri-si-mo-pi-í-te af-tó?)

316. Are there any size options available?
Υπάρχουν διαθέσιμα διαφορετικά μεγέθη;
(I-pár-houn di-a-thé-si-ma di-a-fo-re-ti-ká me-gé-thi?)

317. Can you describe the features of this product?
Μπορείτε να περιγράψετε τα χαρακτηριστικά αυτού του προϊόντος;
(Bo-ree-te na pe-ri-grá-pse-te ta ha-rak-ti-ri-sti-ká af-tú tou pro-í-on-tos?)

Payments

318. I'd like to pay with a credit card.
Θα ήθελα να πληρώσω με πιστωτική κάρτα.
(Tha í-the-la na pli-ró-so me pis-to-ti-kí kár-ta.)

319.   Do you accept debit cards?
        Δέχεστε χρεωστικές κάρτες;
        (Dé-he-ste hre-o-sti-kés kár-tes?)

320.   Can I pay in cash?
        Μπορώ να πληρώσω με μετρητά;
        (Bo-ró na pli-ró-so me me-tri-tá?)

                Idiomatic Expression: "Παίζω με τη φωτιά." -
                Meaning: "Playing with fire (taking a big risk)."
                (Literal translation: "I play with the fire.")

321.   What's your preferred payment method?
        Ποιος είναι ο προτιμώμενος τρόπος πληρωμής σας;
        (Pee-os í-ne o pro-ti-mó-me-nos tró-pos pli-ro-mís sas?)

322.   Is there an extra charge for using a card?
        Υπάρχει επιπλέον χρέωση για τη χρήση κάρτας;
        (I-pár-hi e-pi-plé-on hré-o-si yia ti hrí-si kár-tas?)

323.   Can I split the payment into installments?
        Μπορώ να διαιρέσω την πληρωμή σε δόσεις;
        (Bo-ró na di-ai-ré-so tin pli-ro-mí se dó-sis?)

324.   Do you offer online payment options?
        Προσφέρετε επιλογές πληρωμής διαδικτυακά;
        (Pro-sfé-re-te e-pi-lo-gés pli-ro-mís di-a-dik-ti-a-ká?)

325.   Can I get a receipt for this purchase?
        Μπορώ να πάρω απόδειξη για αυτή την αγορά;
        (Bo-ró na pá-ro a-pó-di-xi yia af-tí tin a-go-rá?)

326. Are there any additional fees?
Υπάρχουν επιπλέον τέλη;
(I-pár-houn e-pi-plé-on té-li?)

327. Is there a minimum purchase amount for card payments?
Υπάρχει ελάχιστο ποσό για πληρωμές με κάρτα;
(I-pár-hi e-lá-his-to po-só yia pli-ro-més me kár-ta?)

> **Travel Story:** On the island of Corfu, a local fisherman said, "Η θάλασσα είναι η ζωή μας," translating to "The sea is our life," reflecting the islanders' deep connection with the sea.

Asking for Recommendations

328. Can you recommend something popular?
Μπορείτε να προτείνετε κάτι δημοφιλές;
(Bo-ree-te na pro-tí-ne-te ká-ti di-mo-fi-lés?)

329. What's your best-selling product?
Ποιο είναι το προϊόν με τις περισσότερες πωλήσεις;
(Pi-o í-ne to pro-í-on me tis pe-ris-só-te-res po-lí-seis?)

330. Do you have any customer favorites?
Έχετε κάποια αγαπημένα προϊόντα από τους πελάτες;
(É-he-te ká-pi-a a-ga-pi-mé-na pro-í-on-ta apó tus pe-lá-tes?)

331. Is there a brand you would suggest?
Υπάρχει κάποιο μάρκα που θα προτείνατε;
(I-pár-hi ká-pi-o már-ka pou tha pro-tí-na-te?)

332. Could you point me to high-quality items?
Μπορείτε να με κατευθύνετε προς προϊόντα υψηλής ποιότητας;
(Bo-ree-te na me ka-tef-thí-ne-te pros pro-í-on-ta ip-si-lís pi-ó-ti-tas?)

333. What do most people choose in this category?
Τι επιλέγουν οι περισσότεροι σε αυτή την κατηγορία;
(Ti e-pi-lé-goun i pe-ris-só-te-roi se af-tí tin ka-ti-go-rí-a?)

334. Are there any special recommendations?
Υπάρχουν κάποιες ιδιαίτερες συστάσεις;
(I-pár-houn ká-pi-es i-di-é-te-res sy-stá-sis?)

335. Can you tell me what's trendy right now?
Μπορείτε να μου πείτε τι είναι της μόδας τώρα;
(Bo-ree-te na mou peí-te ti í-ne tis mó-das tó-ra?)

336. What's your personal favorite here?
Ποιο είναι το προσωπικό σας αγαπημένο εδώ;
(Pi-o í-ne to pro-so-pi-kó sas a-ga-pi-mé-no e-dó?)

337. Any suggestions for a gift?
Έχετε κάποιες προτάσεις για δώρο;
(É-he-te ká-pi-es pro-tá-sis yia dó-ro?)

> **Language Learning Tip:** Immerse Yourself - Full immersion is the most comprehensive way to learn a language.

Returns and Exchanges

338. I'd like to return this item.
Θα ήθελα να επιστρέψω αυτό το προϊόν.
(*Tha í-the-la na e-pi-strép-so af-tó to pro-í-on.*)

339. Can I exchange this for a different size?
Μπορώ να το αλλάξω για διαφορετικό μέγεθος;
(*Bo-ró na to a-lá-xo yia di-a-fo-re-ti-kó mé-ge-thos?*)

340. What's your return policy?
Ποια είναι η πολιτική σας για τις επιστροφές;
(*Pee-a í-ne i po-li-ti-kí sas yia tis e-pi-stro-fés?*)

341. Is there a time limit for returns?
Υπάρχει χρονικό όριο για τις επιστροφές;
(*I-pár-hi hro-ni-kó ó-ri-o yia tis e-pi-stro-fés?*)

342. Do I need a receipt for a return?
Χρειάζεται απόδειξη για την επιστροφή;
(*Hriá-ze-tai a-pó-di-xi yia tin e-pi-stro-fí?*)

343. Is there a restocking fee for returns?
Υπάρχει χρέωση επανατοποθέτησης για τις επιστροφές;
(*I-pár-hi hré-o-si e-pa-na-to-po-thé-ti-sis yia tis e-pi-stro-fés?*)

344. Can I get a refund or store credit?
Μπορώ να λάβω επιστροφή χρημάτων ή πιστωτικό κουπόνι του καταστήματος;
(*Bo-ró na lá-vo e-pi-stro-fí hri-má-ton í pi-sto-ti-kó kou-pó-ni tou ka-ta-stí-ma-tos?*)

45. Do you offer exchanges without receipts?
Προσφέρετε ανταλλαγές χωρίς απόδειξη;
(Pro-sfé-re-te an-ta-la-gés ho-rís a-pó-di-xi?)

46. What's the process for returning a defective item?
Ποια είναι η διαδικασία για την επιστροφή ελαττωματικού προϊόντος;
(Pee-a í-ne i di-a-di-ka-sí-a yia tin e-pi-stro-fí e-lat-to-ma-ti-kú pro-í-on-tos?)

47. Can I return an online purchase in-store?
Μπορώ να επιστρέψω μια αγορά από το διαδίκτυο στο φυσικό κατάστημα;
(Bo-ró na e-pi-strép-so mia a-go-rá apó to di-a-dík-tio sto fi-si-kó ka-tá-sti-ma?)

> Travel Story: In a pottery workshop in Sifnos, the artist said, "Η τέχνη δεν έχει σύνορα," meaning "Art has no borders," celebrating the universal language of creativity.

Shopping for Souvenirs

348. I'm looking for local souvenirs.
Ψάχνω για τοπικά σουβενίρ.
(Psa-hno yia to-pi-ká sou-ve-nír.)

349. What's a popular souvenir from this place?
Ποιο είναι ένα δημοφιλές σουβενίρ από αυτόν τον τόπο;
(Pi-o í-ne é-na di-mo-fi-lés sou-ve-nír apó af-tón ton tó-po?)

350. Do you have any handmade souvenirs?
Έχετε χειροποίητα σουβενίρ;
(É-he-te hi-ro-pí-i-ta sou-ve-nír?)

351. Are there any traditional items here?
     Υπάρχουν εδώ παραδοσιακά αντικείμενα;
     (*I-pár-houn e-dó pa-ra-do-si-a-ká an-ti-kí-me-na?*)

352. Can you suggest a unique souvenir?
     Μπορείτε να προτείνετε ένα μοναδικό σουβενίρ;
     (*Bo-ree-te na pro-tí-ne-te é-na mo-na-di-kó sou-ve-nír?*)

353. I want something that represents this city.
     Θέλω κάτι που αντιπροσωπεύει αυτή την πόλη.
     (*Thé-lo ká-ti pou an-ti-pro-so-pé-vei af-tí tin pó-li.*)

354. Are there souvenirs for a specific landmark?
     Υπάρχουν σουβενίρ για κάποιο συγκεκριμένο αξιοθέατο;
     (*I-pár-houn sou-ve-nír yia ká-pio sing-ke-kri-mé-no
     a-xio-thé-a-to?*)

355. Can you show me souvenirs with cultural significance?
     Μπορείτε να μου δείξετε σουβενίρ με πολιτισμική σημασία;
     (*Bo-ree-te na mou dí-xe-te sou-ve-nír me po-li-tis-mi-kí
     si-ma-sí-a?*)

356. Do you offer personalized souvenirs?
     Προσφέρετε προσωποποιημένα σουβενίρ;
     (*Pro-sfé-re-te pro-so-po-poi-i-mé-na sou-ve-nír?*)

357. What's the price range for souvenirs?
     Ποια είναι η εύρος τιμών για τα σουβενίρ;
     (*Pi-a í-ne i é-vros ti-món yia ta sou-ve-nír?*)

Shopping Online

358. How do I place an order online?
Πώς μπορώ να κάνω παραγγελία διαδικτυακά;
(*Pós bo-ró na ká-no pa-ran-ge-lí-a di-a-dik-ti-a-ká?*)

359. What's the website for online shopping?
Ποια είναι η ιστοσελίδα για διαδικτυακές αγορές;
(*Pi-a í-ne i is-to-se-lí-da yia di-a-dik-ti-a-kés a-go-rés?*)

360. Do you offer free shipping?
Προσφέρετε δωρεάν αποστολή;
(*Pro-sfé-re-te do-re-án a-po-sto-lí?*)

361. Are there any online discounts or promotions?
Υπάρχουν διαδικτυακές εκπτώσεις ή προσφορές;
(*I-pár-houn di-a-dik-ti-a-kés ek-ptó-seis í pro-sfo-rés?*)

362. Can I track my online order?
Μπορώ να παρακολουθήσω την διαδικτυακή μου παραγγελία;
(*Bo-ró na pa-ra-ko-lou-thí-so tin di-a-dik-ti-a-kí mou pa-ran-ge-lí-a?*)

363. What's the return policy for online purchases?
Ποια είναι η πολιτική επιστροφών για διαδικτυακές αγορές;
(*Pi-a í-ne i po-li-ti-kí e-pi-stro-fón yia di-a-dik-ti-a-kés a-go-rés?*)

364. Do you accept various payment methods online?
Δέχεστε διάφορες μεθόδους πληρωμής διαδικτυακά;
(*Dé-he-ste diá-fo-res me-thó-dous pli-ro-mís di-a-dik-ti-a-ká?*)

365.   Is there a customer support hotline for online orders?
Υπάρχει γραμμή υποστήριξης πελατών για διαδικτυακές παραγγελίες;
(*I-pár-hi gra-mí i-po-stí-ri-xis pe-la-tón yia di-a-dik-ti-a-kés pa-ran-ge-lí-es?*)

> **Idiomatic Expression:** "Πέφτω από τα σύννεφα." - Meaning: "To be taken by surprise."
> (Literal translation: "I fall from the clouds.")

366.   Can I change or cancel my online order?
Μπορώ να αλλάξω ή να ακυρώσω την διαδικτυακή μου παραγγελία;
(*Bo-ró na a-lá-xo í na a-ki-ró-so tin di-a-dik-ti-a-kí mou pa-ran-ge-lí-a?*)

367.   What's the delivery time for online purchases?
Πόσο χρόνο διαρκεί η παράδοση για τις διαδικτυακές αγορές;
(*Pó-so hró-no di-ar-kí i pa-rá-do-si yia tis di-a-dik-ti-a-kés a-go-rés?*)

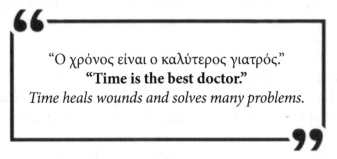

"Ο χρόνος είναι ο καλύτερος γιατρός."
"Time is the best doctor."
Time heals wounds and solves many problems.

Cross Word Puzzle: Shopping

(Provide the English translation for the following Greek words)

Down	Across
1. - ΜΠΟΥΤΙΚ	3. - ΚΑΡΟΤΣΙ
2. - ΠΕΛΆΤΗΣ	5. - ΡΟΎΧΑ
4. - ΛΙΑΝΙΚΉ ΠΏΛΗΣΗ	6. - ΈΚΠΤΩΣΗ
5. - ΤΑΜΊΑΣ	7. - ΑΠΌΔΕΙΞΗ
8. - ΑΓΟΡΈΣ	8. - ΕΚΠΤΩΣΗ
10. - ΤΙΜΉ	9. - ΚΟΥΝΤΕΡ
	11. - ΜΑΡΚΑ
	12. - ΠΟΡΤΟΦΌΛΙ

Correct Answers:

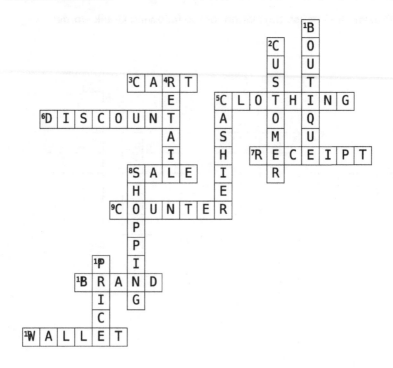

EMERGENCIES

- SEEKING HELP IN CASE OF AN EMERGENCY -
- REPORTING ACCIDENTS OR HEALTH ISSUES -
- CONTACTING AUTHORITIES OR MEDICAL SERVICES -

Getting Help in Emergencies

368. Call an ambulance, please.
      Καλέστε ασθενοφόρο, παρακαλώ.
      (Ka-lé-ste as-the-no-fó-ro, pa-ra-ka-ló.)

> **Language Learning Tip:** Use Greek Subtitles - Watching
> English movies with Greek subtitles can help associate
> words with their meanings.

369. I need a doctor right away.
      Χρειάζομαι γιατρό αμέσως.
      (Hri-á-zo-mai yia-tró a-mé-sos.)

370. Is there a hospital nearby?
      Υπάρχει κοντινό νοσοκομείο;
      (I-pár-hi kon-ti-nó no-so-ko-mí-o?)

371. Help! I've lost my way.
      Βοήθεια! Έχω χαθεί.
      (Vo-í-thei-a! É-ho ha-thí.)

372. Can you call the police?
      Μπορείτε να καλέσετε την αστυνομία;
      (Bo-rí-te na ka-lé-se-te tin as-ty-no-mí-a?)

373. Someone, please call for help.
      Κάποιος, παρακαλώ καλέστε για βοήθεια.
      (Ká-pi-os, pa-ra-ka-ló ka-lé-ste ya vo-í-thei-a.)

374. My friend is hurt, we need assistance.
      Ο φίλος μου είναι τραυματισμένος, χρειαζόμαστε βοήθεια.
      *(O fí-los mou í-ne tra-vma-tis-mé-nos, hri-a-zó-ma-ste
      vo-í-thei-a.)*

375. I've been robbed; I need the authorities.
      Με έχουν ληστέψει· χρειάζομαι τις αρχές.
      (Me é-houn li-sté-psei; hri-á-zo-mai tis ar-hés.)

376. Please, I need immediate assistance.
      Παρακαλώ, χρειάζομαι άμεση βοήθεια.
      (Pa-ra-ka-ló, hri-á-zo-mai á-me-si vo-í-thei-a.)

377. Is there a fire station nearby?
      Υπάρχει κοντινός πυροσβεστικός σταθμός;
      (I-pár-hi kon-ti-nós pi-ro-sves-ti-kós sta-thmós?)

Reporting Incidents

378. I've witnessed an accident.
      Έχω γίνει μάρτυρας ενός ατυχήματος.
      (É-ho gí-nei már-ti-ras e-nós a-ty-hí-ma-tos.)

379. There's been a car crash.
      Έχει συμβεί τροχαίο ατύχημα.
      (É-hi sim-ví tro-hé-o a-ty-hí-ma.)

380. We need to report a fire.
      Πρέπει να αναφέρουμε μια πυρκαγιά.
      (Pré-pi na a-na-fé-rou-me mi-a pir-ka-yi-á.)

381. Someone has stolen my wallet.
      Κάποιος μου έκλεψε το πορτοφόλι.
      (Ká-pi-os mou é-klep-se to por-to-fó-li.)

382. I need to report a lost passport.
Πρέπει να αναφέρω ένα χαμένο διαβατήριο.
(Pré-pei na a-na-fé-ro é-na ha-mé-no dia-va-tí-rio.)

383. There's a suspicious person here.
Υπάρχει εδώ ένας ύποπτος άνθρωπος.
(I-pár-hi e-dó é-nas íp-op-tos án-thro-pos.)

384. I've found a lost child.
Βρήκα ένα χαμένο παιδί.
(Vrí-ka é-na ha-mé-no pe-di.)

385. Can you help me report a missing person?
Μπορείτε να με βοηθήσετε να αναφέρω έναν αγνοούμενο;
(Bo-rí-te na me vo-i-thí-se-te na a-na-fé-ro é-nan a-gno-ú-me-no?)

386. We've had a break-in at our home.
Υπήρξε διάρρηξη στο σπίτι μας.
(I-pír-xe di-ár-ri-xi sto spí-ti mas.)

387. I need to report a damaged vehicle.
Πρέπει να αναφέρω ένα κατεστραμμένο όχημα.
(Pré-pei na a-na-fé-ro é-na ka-te-stram-mé-no ó-hi-ma.)

Contacting Authorities

388. I'd like to speak to the police.
Θέλω να μιλήσω με την αστυνομία.
(Thé-lo na mi-lí-so me tin as-ty-no-mí-a.)

389. I need to contact the embassy.
      Πρέπει να επικοινωνήσω με την πρεσβεία.
      (*Pré-pei na e-pi-ko-i-no-ní-so me tin pre-sveí-a.*)

390. Can you connect me to the fire department?
      Μπορείτε να με συνδέσετε με την πυροσβεστική;
      (*Bo-rí-te na me syn-dé-se-te me tin pi-ro-sves-ti-kí?*)

391. We need to reach animal control.
      Χρειαζόμαστε να φτάσουμε στην υπηρεσία ελέγχου ζώων.
      (*Hri-a-zó-ma-ste na ftá-sou-me stin i-pi-re-sí-a e-lé-hou zó-on.*)

392. How do I get in touch with the coast guard?
      Πώς μπορώ να επικοινωνήσω με την ακτοφυλακή;
      (*Pós bo-ró na e-pi-ko-i-no-ní-so me tin ak-to-fy-la-kí?*)

393. I'd like to report a noise complaint.
      Θέλω να καταγγείλω μια καταγγελία για θόρυβο.
      (*Thé-lo na ka-tan-ghí-lo mi-a ka-tan-ghelí-a gia thó-ri-vo.*)

394. I need to contact child protective services.
      Πρέπει να επικοινωνήσω με τις υπηρεσίες προστασίας των
      παιδιών.
      (*Pré-pei na e-pi-ko-i-no-ní-so me tis i-pi-re-sí-es pro-sta-sí-as ton
      pe-di-on.*)

395. Is there a hotline for disaster relief?
      Υπάρχει γραμμή βοήθειας για καταστροφές;
      (*I-pár-hi gra-mí vo-í-thei-as gia ka-ta-stro-fés?*)

      Fun Fact: The Greek flag has nine stripes, representing
      the nine syllables of the phrase "Eleftheria i Thanatos"
      (Freedom or Death).

396. I want to report a hazardous situation.
Θέλω να αναφέρω μια επικίνδυνη κατάσταση.
(*Thé-lo na a-na-fé-ro mi-a e-pi-kín-di-ni ka-tás-ta-si.*)

397. I need to reach the environmental agency.
Χρειάζομαι να επικοινωνήσω με την υπηρεσία περιβάλλοντος.
(*Hriá-zo-mai na e-pi-ko-i-no-ní-so me tin i-pi-re-sí-a pe-ri-vál-lon-tos.*)

> Travel Story: At a street performance in Athens, an actor exclaimed, "Το θέατρο είναι ο καθρέφτης της ζωής," which means "Theater is the mirror of life."

Medical Emergencies

398. I'm feeling very ill.
Αισθάνομαι πολύ άρρωστος/άρρωστη.
(*Ees-thá-no-mai po-lí ár-ros-tos/ár-ros-ti.*)

399. There's been an accident; we need a medic.
Έγινε ένα ατύχημα· χρειαζόμαστε έναν γιατρό.
(*É-gi-ne é-na a-tí-hi-ma; hri-a-zó-ma-ste é-nan gia-tró.*)

400. Call 112; it's a medical emergency.
Καλέστε το 112· είναι ιατρική έκτακτη ανάγκη.
(*Ka-lé-ste to é-na é-na dío; í-ne ia-tri-kí ék-tak-ti a-nán-gi.*)

> Fun Fact: The Greek alphabet has 24 letters, and it was developed around the 9th century BC.

01. We need an ambulance right away.
     Χρειαζόμαστε ασθενοφόρο αμέσως.
     (Hri-a-zó-ma-ste as-the-no-fó-ro a-mé-sos.)

02. I'm having trouble breathing.
     Έχω πρόβλημα με την αναπνοή.
     (É-ho pró-vli-ma me tin a-na-pno-í.)

03. Someone has lost consciousness.
     Κάποιος έχασε τις αισθήσεις του.
     (Ká-pi-os é-ha-se tis es-thí-seis tou.)

04. I think it's a heart attack; call for help.
     Νομίζω ότι είναι έμφραγμα· καλέστε για βοήθεια.
     (No-mí-zo ó-ti í-ne ém-fra-gma; ka-lé-ste gia vo-í-thei-a.)

05. There's been a severe injury.
     Έχει γίνει σοβαρός τραυματισμός.
     (É-hei gí-nei so-va-rós trav-ma-tis-mós.)

06. I need immediate medical attention.
     Χρειάζομαι άμεση ιατρική προσοχή.
     (Hriá-zo-mai á-me-si ia-tri-kí pro-so-hí.)

07. Is there a first-aid station nearby?
     Υπάρχει κοντά σταθμός πρώτων βοηθειών;
     (I-pár-hi kon-tá sta-thmós pró-ton voi-thei-ón?)

> **Idiomatic Expression:** "Πίνω το αίμα μου." -
> Meaning: "I'm suffering deeply."
> (Literal translation: "I drink my blood.")

Fire and Safety

408.   There's a fire; call 112!
       Υπάρχει φωτιά· καλέστε το 112!
       (I-pár-hi fo-tiá; ka-lé-ste to é-na é-na dío!)

409.   We need to evacuate the building.
       Πρέπει να εκκενώσουμε το κτίριο.
       (Pré-pi na ek-ke-nó-soo-me to k-tí-rio.)

410.   Fire extinguisher, quick!
       Πυροσβεστήρας, γρήγορα!
       (Pi-ro-sve-stí-ras, grí-go-ra!)

411.   I smell gas; we need to leave.
       Μυρίζω αέριο· πρέπει να φύγουμε.
       (Mi-rí-zo aé-rio; pré-pi na fí-gou-me.)

> **Fun Fact:** The philosophers of ancient Greece, including
> Aristotle, used to teach while walking. This was known
> as peripatetic philosophy.

412.   Can you contact the fire department?
       Μπορείτε να επικοινωνήσετε με την πυροσβεστική;
       (Bo-rí-te na e-pi-ko-i-no-ní-se-te me tin pi-ro-sve-sti-kí?)

413.   There's a hazardous spill; we need help.
       Υπάρχει επικίνδυνη διαρροή· χρειαζόμαστε βοήθεια.
       (I-pár-hi e-pi-kín-di-ni di-a-ró-i; hri-a-zó-ma-ste vo-í-thei-a.)

414.   Is there a fire escape route?
       Υπάρχει διαδρομή διαφυγής από φωτιά;
       (I-pár-hi di-a-dro-mí di-a-fi-gís a-pó fo-tiá?)

415. This area is not safe; we need to move.
Αυτή η περιοχή δεν είναι ασφαλής· πρέπει να κινηθούμε.
(*Af-tí i pe-ri-o-hí den í-ne as-fa-lís; pré-pi na ki-ni-thóu-me.*)

416. Alert, there's a potential explosion.
Προσοχή, υπάρχει πιθανότητα έκρηξης.
(*Pro-so-hí, i-pár-hi pi-tha-nó-ti-ta ék-ri-xis.*)

417. I see smoke; we need assistance.
Βλέπω καπνό· χρειαζόμαστε βοήθεια.
(*Vlé-po kap-nó; hri-a-zó-ma-ste vo-í-thei-a.*)

Natural Disasters

418. It's an earthquake; take cover!
Είναι σεισμός· βρείτε καταφύγιο!
(*Í-ne si-smós; vreí-te ka-ta-fí-gio!*)

419. We're experiencing a tornado; find shelter.
Βιώνουμε έναν ανεμοστρόβιλο· βρείτε καταφύγιο.
(*Vió-nou-me é-nan a-ne-mo-stró-vi-lo; vreí-te ka-ta-fí-gio.*)

420. Flood warning; move to higher ground.
Προειδοποίηση για πλημμύρα· μετακινηθείτε σε υψηλότερο έδαφος.
(*Pro-ei-do-pí-i-si ya plim-mí-ra; me-ta-ki-ni-thí-te se i-psi-ló-te-ro é-da-fos.*)

421. We need to prepare for a hurricane.
Πρέπει να προετοιμαστούμε για τυφώνα.
(*Pré-pi na pro-e-ti-mas-tóu-me ya ti-fó-na.*)

422. This is a tsunami alert; head inland.
Είναι συναγερμός για τσουνάμι· κατευθυνθείτε προς την ενδοχώρα.
(Í-ne si-na-ger-mós ya tsoo-ná-mi; ka-tef-thin-thí-te pros tin en-do-hó-ra.)

Fun Fact: Ancient Athens is considered the birthplace of democracy.

423. It's a wildfire; evacuate immediately.
Πρόκειται για δασική πυρκαγιά· εκκενώστε αμέσως.
(Pró-kei-tai ya da-si-kí pir-ka-gi-á; ek-ke-nó-ste a-mé-sos.)

424. There's a volcanic eruption; take precautions.
Υπάρχει ηφαιστειακή έκρηξη· πάρτε τα μέτρα σας.
(I-pár-hi i-fe-sti-a-kí é-kri-xi; pá-rte ta mé-tra sas.)

425. We've had an avalanche; help needed.
Συνέβη χιονοστιβάδα· χρειαζόμαστε βοήθεια.
(Si-né-vi hio-no-sti-vá-da; hri-a-zó-ma-ste vo-í-thei-a.)

426. Earthquake aftershock; stay indoors.
Μετασεισμός· παραμείνετε μέσα.
(Me-ta-si-smós; pa-ra-mí-ne-te mé-sa.)

427. Severe thunderstorm; seek shelter.
Σφοδρή καταιγίδα· αναζητήστε καταφύγιο.
(Sfo-drí ka-tai-gí-da; a-na-zi-tí-ste ka-ta-fí-gio.)

Emergency Services Information

428. What's the emergency hotline number?
Ποιος είναι ο αριθμός της επείγουσας βοήθειας;
(Pi-os í-ne o a-rith-mós tis e-pí-gou-sas vo-í-thei-as?)

429. Where's the nearest police station?
Πού βρίσκεται ο πλησιέστερος αστυνομικός σταθμός;
(Poú vrí-ske-tai o pli-sié-ste-ros a-sti-no-mi-kós sta-thmós?)

430. How do I contact the fire department?
Πώς μπορώ να επικοινωνήσω με την πυροσβεστική;
(Pós bo-ró na e-pi-ko-i-no-ní-so me tin pi-ro-sve-sti-kí?)

431. Is there a hospital nearby?
Υπάρχει νοσοκομείο κοντά;
(I-pár-hi no-so-ko-mí-o kon-dá?)

432. What's the number for poison control?
Ποιος είναι ο αριθμός για το κέντρο δηλητηριάσεων;
(Pi-os í-ne o a-rith-mós ya to kén-tro di-li-ti-ri-á-se-on?)

433. Where can I find a disaster relief center?
Πού μπορώ να βρω ένα κέντρο αντιμετώπισης καταστροφών;
(Poú bo-ró na vro é-na kén-tro an-ti-me-tó-pi-sis ka-ta-stro-fón?)

> **Fun Fact:** Santorini is known for its stunning sunsets and is home to one of the world's few volcanic calderas in the sea.

434. What's the local emergency radio station?
Ποια είναι ο τοπικός εκτάκτου ανάγκης ραδιοφωνικός σταθμός;
(Pee-ah í-ne o to-pee-kós ek-ták-tou a-nán-kis ra-dee-o-fo-nee-kós sta-thmós?)

435. Are there any shelters in the area?
Υπάρχουν καταφύγια στην περιοχή;
(I-pár-houn ka-ta-fí-yia stin pe-ree-o-hí?)

436. Who do I call for road assistance?
Σε ποιον απευθύνομαι για οδική βοήθεια;
(Se pee-on a-ef-thí-no-meh ya o-thee-kí vo-í-thee-a?)

437. How can I reach search and rescue teams?
Πώς μπορώ να επικοινωνήσω με τις ομάδες αναζήτησης και διάσωσης;
(Pós bo-ró na e-pi-ko-i-no-ní-so me tis o-má-des a-na-zí-ti-sis ke thee-á-so-sis?)

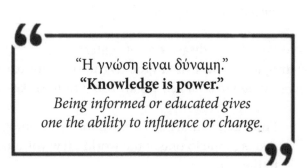

"Η γνώση είναι δύναμη."
"Knowledge is power."
*Being informed or educated gives
one the ability to influence or change.*

Interactive Challenge: Emergencies Quiz

. How do you say "emergency" in Greek?

a) Μήλο
b) Έκτακτη ανάγκη
c) Τυρί
d) Παραλία

. What's the Greek word for "ambulance"?

a) Αυτοκίνητο
b) Ποδήλατο
c) Ασθενοφόρο
d) Σχολείο

. If you need immediate medical attention, what should you say in Greek?

a) Θέλω ψωμί.
b) Πού είναι ο σταθμός;
c) Χρειάζομαι άμεση ιατρική βοήθεια.

. How do you ask "Is there a hospital nearby?" in Greek?

a) Πού είναι το σινεμά;
b) Έχετε στυλό;
c) Υπάρχει νοσοκομείο εδώ κοντά;

. What's the Greek word for "police"?

a) Μήλο
b) Αστυνομία
c) Τρένο

6. How do you say "fire" in Greek?

   a) Ήλιος
   b) Σκύλος
   c) Φωτιά
   d) Βιβλίο

7. If you've witnessed an accident, what phrase can you use in Greek?

   a) Θέλω σοκολάτα.
   b) Είδα ένα ατύχημα.
   c) Μου αρέσουν τα λουλούδια.
   d) Αυτό είναι το σπίτι μου.

8. What's the Greek word for "help"?

   a) Αντίο
   b) Καλημέρα
   c) Ευχαριστώ
   d) Βοήθεια!

9. How would you say "I've been robbed; I need the authorities" in Greek?

   a) Έφαγα τυρί.
   b) Με λήστεψαν· χρειάζομαι τις αρχές.
   c) Αυτό είναι ένα όμορφο βουνό.

10. How do you ask "Can you call an ambulance, please?" in Greek?

   a) Μπορείτε να καλέσετε ένα ταξί, παρακαλώ;
   b) Μπορείτε να μου δώσετε αλάτι;
   c) Μπορείτε να καλέσετε ένα ασθενοφόρο, παρακαλώ;

1. What's the Greek word for "emergency services"?

a) Έκτακτες υπηρεσίες
b) Νόστιμη τούρτα
c) Ελαφρύ

2. How do you say "reporting an accident" in Greek?

a) Τραγουδώ ένα τραγούδι
b) Διαβάζω ένα βιβλίο
c) Αναφορά ατυχήματος

13. If you need to contact the fire department, what should you say in Greek?

a) Πώς πάω στη βιβλιοθήκη;
b) Πρέπει να επικοινωνήσω με την πυροσβεστική.
c) Ψάχνω τον φίλο μου.

14. What's the Greek word for "urgent"?

a) Μικρός
b) Όμορφος
c) Γρήγορος
d) Επείγων

15. How do you ask for the nearest police station in Greek?

a) Πού είναι ο πλησιέστερος φούρνος;
b) Πού είναι ο πλησιέστερος αστυνομικός σταθμός;
c) Έχετε χάρτη;
d) Τι ώρα είναι;

Correct Answers:

1. b)
2. c)
3. c)
4. c)
5. b)
6. c)
7. b)
8. d)
9. b)
10. c)
11. a)
12. c)
13. b)
14. d)
15. b)

EVERYDAY CONVERSATIONS

- SMALL TALK AND CASUAL CONVERSATIONS -
- DISCUSSING THE WEATHER, HOBBIES, AND INTERESTS -
- MAKING PLANS WITH FRIENDS OR ACQUAINTANCES -

Small Talk

438. How's it going?
Πώς πάει;
(Pós pá-ee?)

439. Nice weather we're having, isn't it?
Όμορφος καιρός σήμερα, έτσι δεν είναι;
(Ó-mor-fos ke-rós sí-me-ra, ét-si den í-ne?)

440. Have any exciting plans for the weekend?
Έχετε κάποια συναρπαστικά σχέδια για το σαββατοκύριακο;
(É-che-te ká-pia si-nar-pas-ti-ká sché-di-a ya to sa-va-to-kí-ri-a-ko?)

441. Did you catch that new movie?
Είδατε την καινούργια ταινία;
(Í-da-te tin ke-noú-ri-a te-ní-a?)

442. How's your day been so far?
Πώς πήγε η μέρα σας μέχρι τώρα;
(Pós pí-ge i mé-ra sas mé-hri tó-ra?)

443. What do you do for work?
Τι κάνετε για δουλειά;
(Ti ká-ne-te ya dou-lei-á?)

444. Do you come here often?
Έρχεστε συχνά εδώ;
(Ér-che-ste sih-ná e-dó?)

445. Have you tried the food at this place before?
Έχετε δοκιμάσει πριν το φαγητό εδώ;
(É-che-te do-ki-má-sei prin to fa-yi-tó e-dó?)

46. Any recommendations for things to do in town?
Έχετε καμία σύσταση για δραστηριότητες στην πόλη;
(*É-che-te ka-mí-a sí-sta-si ya dras-ti-ri-ó-ti-tes stin pó-li?*)

47. Do you follow any sports teams?
Ακολουθείτε κάποια αθλητική ομάδα;
(*A-ko-lou-thí-te ká-pia ath-li-ti-kí o-má-da?*)

48. Have you traveled anywhere interesting lately?
Έχετε ταξιδέψει πρόσφατα κάπου ενδιαφέρον;
(*É-che-te ta-xi-dép-si pró-sfa-ta ká-pou en-di-a-fé-ron?*)

49. Do you enjoy cooking?
Σας αρέσει να μαγειρεύετε;
(*Sas a-ré-si na ma-yi-reú-e-te?*)

> **Travel Story:** In a music shop in Crete, the owner played a lyra and said, "Η μουσική ενώνει τις καρδιές," translating to "Music unites hearts."

Casual Conversations

50. What's your favorite type of music?
Ποιο είναι το αγαπημένο σας είδος μουσικής;
(*Pee-o í-ne to a-ga-pi-mé-no sas í-dos mou-si-kís?*)

> **Fun Fact:** Feta, a famous Greek cheese, is made primarily from sheep's milk.

451. How do you like to spend your free time?
Πώς σας αρέσει να περνάτε τον ελεύθερο χρόνο σας;
(Pos-sas-a-re-si-na-per-na-te-ton-e-lef-the-ro-chro-no-sas?)

452. Do you have any pets?
Έχετε κατοικίδια;
(E-che-te-ka-toi-ki-dia?)

453. Where did you grow up?
Πού μεγαλώσατε;
(Pou-me-ga-lo-sa-te?)

454. What's your family like?
Πώς είναι η οικογένειά σας;
(Pos-ei-nai-i-oi-ko-ge-nei-a-sas?)

455. Are you a morning person or a night owl?
Είστε πρωινός τύπος ή νυχτερινός;
(Ei-ste-pro-i-nos-ty-pos-i-nych-te-ri-nos?)

456. Do you prefer coffee or tea?
Προτιμάτε τον καφέ ή το τσάι;
(Pro-ti-ma-te-ton-ka-fe-i-to-tsa-i?)

457. Are you into any TV shows right now?
Βλέπετε κάποια τηλεοπτική σειρά αυτή τη στιγμή;
(Vle-pe-te-ka-poi-a-ti-le-op-ti-ki-sei-ra-af-ti-ti-sti-gmi?)

> **Idiomatic Expression:** "Σπάω το κεφάλι μου." -
> Meaning: "I'm racking my brain."
> (Literal translation: "I break my head.")

158. What's the last book you read?
Ποιο είναι το τελευταίο βιβλίο που διαβάσατε;
(*Pi-o-ei-nai-to-te-lef-ta-io-vi-vli-o-pou-dia-va-sa-te?*)

159. Do you like to travel?
Σας αρέσει να ταξιδεύετε;
(*Sas-a-re-si-na-ta-xi-dev-e-te?*)

160. Are you a fan of outdoor activities?
Σας αρέσουν οι υπαίθριες δραστηριότητες;
(*Sas-a-re-soun-oi-y-pe-thri-es-dras-ti-ri-o-ti-tes?*)

161. How do you unwind after a long day?
Πώς χαλαρώνετε μετά από μια κουραστική μέρα;
(*Pos-cha-la-ro-ne-te-me-ta-a-po-mia-kou-ras-ti-ki-me-ra?*)

Discussing the Weather

462. Can you believe this heat/cold?
Μπορείτε να πιστέψετε αυτή τη ζέστη/κρύο;
(*Mbo-rei-te-na-pi-ste-pse-te-af-ti-ti-zes-ti/kri-o?*)

463. I heard it's going to rain all week.
Άκουσα ότι θα βρέχει όλη την εβδομάδα.
(*A-kou-sa-o-ti-tha-vre-chei-o-li-tin-ev-do-ma-da.*)

464. What's the temperature like today?
Πώς είναι η θερμοκρασία σήμερα;
(*Pos-ei-nai-i-ther-mo-kra-si-a-si-me-ra?*)

465. Do you like sunny or cloudy days better?
Προτιμάτε τις ηλιόλουστες ή τις συννεφιασμένες μέρες;
(Pro-ti-ma-te tis i-li-o-lou-stes i tis syn-ne-fi-as-me-nes me-res?)

466. Have you ever seen a snowstorm like this?
Έχετε δει ποτέ χιονοθύελλα σαν αυτή;
(E-che-te de-i po-te chi-o-no-thy-el-la san af-ti?)

467. Is it always this humid here?
Είναι πάντα τόσο υγρό εδώ;
(Ei-nai pan-ta to-so i-gro e-do?)

468. Did you get caught in that thunderstorm yesterday?
Μπήκατε στη χθεσινή καταιγίδα;
(Bi-ka-te sti chthe-si-ni ka-tai-gi-da?)

469. What's the weather like in your hometown?
Πώς είναι ο καιρός στην πόλη σας;
(Pos ei-nai o ke-ros stin po-li sas?)

470. I can't stand the wind; how about you?
Δεν αντέχω τον άνεμο; Εσείς;
(Den an-te-cho ton a-ne-mo? E-se-is?)

471. Is it true the winters here are mild?
Είναι αλήθεια ότι οι χειμώνες εδώ είναι ήπιοι;
(Ei-nai a-li-theia o-ti oi chi-mo-nes e-do ei-nai i-pi-oi?)

472. Do you like beach weather?
      Σας αρέσει ο καιρός για την παραλία;
      (*Sas a-re-sei o ke-ros gia tin pa-ra-li-a?*)

473. How do you cope with the humidity in summer?
      Πώς αντιμετωπίζετε την υγρασία το καλοκαίρι;
      (*Pos an-ti-me-to-pi-ze-te tin i-gra-si-a to ka-lo-ke-ri?*)

Hobbies

474. What are your hobbies or interests?
      Ποια είναι τα χόμπι ή τα ενδιαφέροντά σας;
      (*Pia ei-nai ta cho-bi i ta en-di-a-fe-ron-ta sas?*)

475. Do you play any musical instruments?
      Παίζετε κάποιο μουσικό όργανο;
      (*Pai-ze-te ka-pio mou-si-ko or-ga-no?*)

476. Have you ever tried painting or drawing?
      Έχετε δοκιμάσει ποτέ το ζωγραφική ή τη σχεδίαση;
      (*E-che-te do-ki-ma-si po-te to zo-gra-fi-ki i ti sche-di-a-si?*)

477. Are you a fan of sports?
      Σας αρέσουν τα αθλήματα;
      (*Sas a-re-soun ta ath-li-ma-ta?*)

478. Do you enjoy cooking or baking?
      Σας αρέσει να μαγειρεύετε ή να ψήνετε;
      (*Sas a-re-sei na ma-yei-rev-e-te i na psee-ne-te?*)

479.   Are you into photography?
        Σας ενδιαφέρει η φωτογραφία;
        (Sas en-di-a-fe-ri i fo-to-gra-fia?)

480.   Have you ever tried gardening?
        Έχετε δοκιμάσει ποτέ την κηπουρική;
        (E-che-te do-ki-ma-si po-te tin ki-pou-ri-ki?)

481.   Do you like to read in your free time?
        Σας αρέσει να διαβάζετε στον ελεύθερο χρόνο σας;
        (Sas a-re-si na di-a-va-zete ston e-lef-the-ro chro-no sas?)

482.   Have you explored any new hobbies lately?
        Έχετε εξερευνήσει κάποια νέα χόμπι τελευταία;
        (E-che-te ex-e-re-vni-si ka-pia ne-a cho-bi te-lef-ta-ia?)

483.   Are you a collector of anything?
        Συλλέγετε κάτι;
        (Sy-le-ge-te ka-ti?)

484.   Do you like to watch movies or TV shows?
        Σας αρέσει να βλέπετε ταινίες ή τηλεοπτικές σειρές;
        (Sas a-re-si na vle-pe-te te-ni-es i ti-le-op-ti-kes si-res?)

485.   Have you ever taken up a craft project?
        Έχετε ασχοληθεί ποτέ με κάποιο χειροτεχνικό έργο;
        (E-che-te as-cho-li-thi po-te me ka-pio chi-ro-tech-ni-ko er-go?)

> **Idiomatic Expression:** "Το έριξα στα βαθιά." -
> Meaning: "I took the plunge."
> (Literal translation: "I threw it into the deep.")

Interests

86. What topics are you passionate about?
Για ποια θέματα έχετε πάθος;
(Gia pi-a the-ma-ta e-che-te pa-thos?)

87. Are you involved in any social causes?
Συμμετέχετε σε κοινωνικές δράσεις;
(Sym-me-te-che-te se ki-no-ni-kes dra-sis?)

88. Do you enjoy learning new languages?
Σας αρέσει να μαθαίνετε νέες γλώσσες;
(Sas a-re-si na ma-the-ne-te ne-es glo-ses?)

89. Are you into fitness or wellness?
Σας ενδιαφέρει η γυμναστική ή η ευεξία;
(Sas en-di-a-fe-ri i gim-na-sti-ki i i e-ve-xi-a?)

90. Are you a technology enthusiast?
Είστε λάτρης της τεχνολογίας;
(Ei-ste la-tris tis tech-no-lo-gi-as?)

91. What's your favorite genre of books or movies?
Ποιο είναι το αγαπημένο σας είδος βιβλίων ή ταινιών;
(Pi-o i-ne to a-ga-pi-me-no sas i-dos vi-vli-on i te-ni-on?)

92. Do you follow current events or politics?
Ακολουθείτε τα τρέχοντα γεγονότα ή την πολιτική;
(A-ko-lou-thi-te ta tre-chon-ta ge-go-no-ta i tin po-li-ti-ki?)

493. Are you into fashion or design?
Σας ενδιαφέρει η μόδα ή ο σχεδιασμός;
(Sas en-di-a-fe-ri i mo-da i o sche-di-as-mos?)

494. Are you a history buff?
Είστε λάτρης της ιστορίας;
(Ee-ste la-tris tis i-sto-ri-as?)

495. Have you ever been involved in volunteer work?
Έχετε ασχοληθεί ποτέ με εθελοντική εργασία;
(E-che-te as-cho-li-thei po-te me e-the-lon-ti-ki er-ga-si-a?)

496. Are you passionate about cooking or food culture?
Σας συγκινεί το μαγείρεμα ή η γαστρονομική κουλτούρα;
(Sas syn-ki-ni to ma-gi-re-ma i i gas-tro-no-mi-ki koul-tou-ra?)

497. Are you an advocate for any specific hobbies or interests?
Υποστηρίζετε κάποια συγκεκριμένα χόμπι ή ενδιαφέροντα;
(Y-po-sti-ri-zete ka-pi-a syn-ke-kri-me-na cho-mbi i en-di-a-fe-ron-ta?)

> **Idiomatic Expression:** "Τρέχω σαν τρελός/τρελή." - Meaning: "Running around like crazy (very busy)." (Literal translation: "I run like a madman/madwoman.")

Making Plans

498. Would you like to grab a coffee sometime?
Θα θέλατε να πιούμε έναν καφέ κάποια στιγμή;
(Tha the-la-te na pi-ou-me e-nan ka-fe ka-pia stig-mi?)

499. Let's plan a dinner outing this weekend.
Ας οργανώσουμε μια βραδινή έξοδο αυτό το σαββατοκύριακο.
(*As or-ga-no-sou-me mia vra-di-ni ex-o-do af-to to sav-va-to-ky-ri-a-ko.*)

500. How about going to a movie on Friday night?
Τι λέτε για μια ταινία την Παρασκευή το βράδυ;
(*Ti le-te gia mia te-ni-a tin Pa-ra-ske-vi to vra-di?*)

501. Do you want to join us for a hike next weekend?
Θέλετε να μας συνοδεύσετε σε μια πεζοπορία το επόμενο σαββατοκύριακο;
(*The-le-te na mas sy-no-de-fse-te se mia pe-zo-po-ri-a to e-po-me-no sav-va-to-ky-ri-a-ko?*)

502. We should organize a game night soon.
Θα έπρεπε να οργανώσουμε μια βραδιά παιχνιδιών σύντομα.
(*Tha e-pre-pe na or-ga-no-sou-me mia vra-di-a pe-chi-di-on syn-to-ma.*)

503. Let's catch up over lunch next week.
Ας βρεθούμε για μεσημεριανό την επόμενη εβδομάδα.
(*As vre-thou-me gia me-si-me-ri-a-no tin e-po-me-ni ev-do-ma-da.*)

504. Would you be interested in a shopping trip?
Θα ενδιαφέρεστε για μια εκδρομή για ψώνια;
(*Tha en-di-a-fe-re-ste gia mia ek-dro-mi gia pso-nia?*)

505. I'm thinking of visiting the museum; care to join?
Σκέφτομαι να επισκεφτώ το μουσείο· θέλετε να έρθετε;
(*Skef-to-mai na e-pi-skef-to to mou-sei-o; the-le-te na er-the-te?*)

506. How about a picnic in the park?
Τι λες για ένα πικνίκ στο πάρκο;
(*Ti les gia ena pik-nik sto par-ko?*)

> **Fun Fact:** Originally, the iconic white marble statues of ancient Greece were brightly painted.

507. Let's get together for a study session.
Ας συναντηθούμε για μια συνεδρία μελέτης.
(*As sy-nan-ti-thou-me gia mia sy-ne-dri-a me-le-tis.*)

508. We should plan a beach day this summer.
Θα πρέπει να οργανώσουμε μια μέρα στην παραλία αυτό το καλοκαίρι.
(*Tha pre-pei na or-ga-no-sou-me mia me-ra stin pa-ra-li-a af-to to ka-lo-kai-ri.*)

509. Want to come over for a barbecue at my place?
Θέλεις να έρθεις για μπάρμπεκιου στο σπίτι μου;
(*The-leis na er-theis gia bar-mpe-kiou sto spi-ti mou?*)

"Κάθε αρχή και δύσκολη."
"Every beginning is difficult."
Starting something new often comes with challenges.

Interactive Challenge: Everyday Conversations
(Link each English word with their corresponding meaning in Greek)

1) Conversation	Ανταλλαγή Απόψεων
2) Greeting	Χαιρετισμός
3) Question	Συζήτηση
4) Answer	Κουβεντούλα
5) Salutation	Διάλογος
6) Communication	Απάντηση
7) Dialogue	Ομιλία
8) Small Talk	Επικοινωνία
9) Discussion	Συζήτηση
10) Speech	Γλώσσα
11) Language	Κοινή Χρήση Ιδεών
12) Exchange of Opinions	Έκφραση
13) Expression	Ερώτηση
14) Casual Conversation	Ανεπίσημη Συζήτηση
15) Sharing Ideas	Χαιρετισμός

Correct Answers:

1. Conversation - Συζήτηση
2. Greeting - Χαιρετισμός
3. Question - Ερώτηση
4. Answer - Απάντηση
5. Salutation - Χαιρετισμός
6. Communication - Επικοινωνία
7. Dialogue - Διάλογος
8. Small Talk - Κουβεντούλα
9. Discussion - Συζήτηση
10. Speech - Ομιλία
11. Language - Γλώσσα
12. Exchange of Opinions - Ανταλλαγή Απόψεων
13. Expression - Έκφραση
14. Casual Conversation - Ανεπίσημη Συζήτηση
15. Sharing Ideas - Κοινή Χρήση Ιδεών

BUSINESS & WORK

INTRODUCING YOURSELF IN A PROFESSIONAL SETTING -
- DISCUSSING WORK-RELATED TOPICS -
- NEGOTIATING BUSINESS DEALS OR CONTRACTS -

Professional Introductions

510.   Hi, I'm [Your Name].
       Γεια, είμαι ο/η [Το Όνομά σας].
       (Yi-a, ei-mai o/i [To O-no-ma sas].)

511.   What do you do for a living?
       Τι κάνετε για δουλειά;
       (Ti ka-ne-te yia dou-lei-a?)

512.   What's your role in the company?
       Ποια είναι η θέση σας στην εταιρεία;
       (Pi-a ei-nai i the-si sas stin e-tai-ri-a?)

513.   Can you tell me about your background?
       Μπορείτε να μου πείτε κάτι για το επαγγελματικό σας υπόβαθρο;
       (Bo-rei-te na mou pei-te ka-ti yia to e-pag-ge-lma-ti-ko sas y-po-va-thro?)

514.   Are you familiar with our team?
       Γνωρίζετε την ομάδα μας;
       (Gno-ri-ze-te tin o-ma-da mas?)

515.   May I introduce myself?
       Μπορώ να συστηθώ;
       (Bo-ro na sy-sti-tho?)

516.   I work in [Your Department].
       Δουλεύω στο [Το Τμήμα σας].
       (Dou-le-vo sto [To Tmi-ma sas].)

517.   How long have you been with the company?
       Πόσο καιρό είστε στην εταιρεία;
       (Po-so kai-ro eis-te stin e-tai-ri-a?)

518. This is my colleague, [Colleague's Name].
      Αυτός/Αυτή είναι ο/η συνάδελφός μου, [Όνομα Συναδέλφου].
      *(Af-tos/Af-ti ei-nai o/i sy-nad-el-fos mou, [O-no-ma
      Sy-na-del-fou].)*

519. Let me introduce you to our manager.
      Επιτρέψτε μου να σας συστήσω στον διευθυντή μας.
      (E-pi-trep-ste mou na sas sy-sti-so ston di-ef-thyn-ti mas.)

      Travel Story: On a hiking trail in Samaria Gorge, a
      fellow hiker said, "Το μονοπάτι είναι η απάντηση,"
      meaning "The path is the answer," emphasizing the
      journey's importance.

Work Conversations

520. Can we discuss the project?
      Μπορούμε να συζητήσουμε το έργο;
      (Bo-rou-me na sy-zi-ti-sou-me to er-go?)

521. Let's go over the details.
      Ας αναλύσουμε τις λεπτομέρειες.
      (As a-na-ly-so-u-me tis lep-to-me-ri-es.)

522. What's the agenda for the meeting?
      Ποια είναι η ατζέντα της συνάντησης;
      (Pi-a ei-nai i at-zen-ta tis sy-nan-ti-sis?)

523. I'd like your input on this.
      Θα ήθελα την άποψή σας σε αυτό.
      (Tha i-the-la tin a-po-psi sas se af-to.)

524. We need to address this issue.
      Πρέπει να ασχοληθούμε με αυτό το πρόβλημα.
      (Pre-pei na as-cho-li-thou-me me af-to to pro-vli-ma.)

525. How's the project progressing?
      Πώς προχωράει το έργο;
      (Pos pro-cho-ra-i to er-go?)

526. Do you have any updates for me?
      Έχετε κάποιες ενημερώσεις για μένα;
      (E-che-te ka-pi-es e-ni-me-ro-seis gia me-na?)

527. Let's brainstorm some ideas.
      Ας διατυπώσουμε κάποιες ιδέες.
      (As dia-ti-po-sou-me ka-pi-es i-de-es.)

528. Can we schedule a team meeting?
      Μπορούμε να προγραμματίσουμε μια ομαδική συνάντηση;
      (Bo-rou-me na pro-gram-ma-ti-sou-me mia o-ma-di-ki sy-nan-ti-si?)

529. I'm open to suggestions.
      Είμαι ανοιχτός σε προτάσεις.
      (Ei-mai a-nih-tos se pro-ta-sis.)

Business Negotiations

530. We need to negotiate the terms.
      Πρέπει να διαπραγματευτούμε τους όρους.
      (Pre-pei na dia-prag-ma-tef-tou-me tous o-rous.)

531. What's your offer?
Ποια είναι η προσφορά σας;
(Pi-a ei-nai i pro-sfo-ra sas?)

532. Can we find a middle ground?
Μπορούμε να βρούμε μέση οδό;
(Bo-rou-me na vroo-me me-si o-do?)

> **Idiomatic Expression:** "Βγήκε ο ήλιος στην καρδιά μου."
> - Meaning: "My heart is filled with joy."
> (Literal translation: "The sun came out in my heart.")

533. Let's discuss the contract.
Ας συζητήσουμε το συμβόλαιο.
(As sy-zi-ti-sou-me to sym-vo-lai-o.)

534. Are you flexible on the price?
Είστε ευέλικτοι στην τιμή;
(Eis-te ev-eli-ktoi stin ti-mi?)

535. I'd like to propose a deal.
Θα ήθελα να προτείνω μια συμφωνία.
(Tha i-the-la na pro-ti-no mia sym-fo-ni-a.)

536. We're interested in your terms.
Ενδιαφερόμαστε για τους όρους σας.
(En-di-a-fe-ro-mas-te gia tous o-rous sas.)

537. Can we talk about the agreement?
Μπορούμε να συζητήσουμε για τη συμφωνία;
(Bo-rou-me na sy-zi-ti-sou-me gia ti sym-fo-ni-a?)

> **Fun Fact:** The shipwreck on Navagio Beach in Zakynthos makes it one of the most photographed spots in Greece.

538. Let's work out the details.
Ας διευκρινίσουμε τις λεπτομέρειες.
(*As di-ev-kri-ni-soo-me tis lep-to-me-ri-ees.*)

539. What are your conditions?
Ποιες είναι οι προϋποθέσεις σας;
(*Pee-es ee-nai ee pro-i-poth-ee-sis sas?*)

540. We should reach a compromise.
Πρέπει να φτάσουμε σε συμβιβασμό.
(*Pre-pei na fta-soo-me se sym-vi-vas-mo.*)

> **Fun Fact:** Greece won the Eurovision Song Contest for the first time in 2005 with Helena Paparizou's "My Number One".

Workplace Etiquette

541. Remember to be punctual.
Να θυμάστε να είστε έγκαιροι.
(*Na thi-mas-te na ee-ste eng-ke-roi.*)

542. Always maintain a professional demeanor.
Διατηρήστε πάντα επαγγελματική στάση.
(*Diat-i-ri-ste pan-da e-pag-el-ma-ti-ki sta-si.*)

543. Respect your colleagues' personal space.
Σεβαστείτε τον προσωπικό χώρο των συναδέλφων σας.
(*Se-vas-ti-te ton pro-so-pi-ko cho-ro ton si-na-del-fon sas.*)

> **Fun Fact:** Ikaria is known as one of the world's "Blue Zones" where people live significantly longer than average.

44. Dress appropriately for the office.
Ντυθείτε κατάλληλα για το γραφείο.
(*Ndi-thei-te ka-tal-la gia to gra-fi-o.*)

45. Follow company policies and guidelines.
Ακολουθήστε τις πολιτικές και τις οδηγίες της εταιρείας.
(*A-ko-lou-thi-ste tis po-li-ti-kes ke tis o-di-gi-es tis e-te-ri-as.*)

46. Use respectful language in conversations.
Χρησιμοποιήστε ευγενική γλώσσα στις συνομιλίες.
(*Chri-si-mo-poi-i-ste ev-gen-i-ki glo-ssa stis si-no-mi-lies.*)

47. Keep your workspace organized.
Κρατήστε τον χώρο εργασίας σας οργανωμένο.
(*Kra-ti-ste ton cho-ro er-ga-si-as sas or-ga-no-me-no.*)

48. Be mindful of office noise levels.
Να είστε προσεκτικοί στα επίπεδα θορύβου στο γραφείο.
(*Na ee-ste pro-sek-ti-koi sta e-pi-pe-da tho-ry-vou sto gra-fi-o.*)

49. Offer assistance when needed.
Προσφέρετε βοήθεια όταν χρειάζεται.
(*Pro-sfe-re-te vo-i-thei-a o-tan chre-i-a-ze-tai.*)

50. Practice good hygiene at work.
Διατηρείτε καλή υγιεινή στην εργασία.
(*Diat-i-ri-te ka-li yi-gi-i-ni stin er-ga-si-a.*)

51. Avoid office gossip and rumors.
Αποφεύγετε τα κουτσομπολιά και τις φήμες στο γραφείο.
(*A-po-fev-ge-te ta kout-so-bo-li-a ke tis fi-mes sto gra-fi-o.*)

Job Interviews

552.   Tell me about yourself.
       Πες μου κάτι για εσένα.
       (Pes moo kah-tee yia eh-seh-nah.)

553.   What are your strengths and weaknesses?
       Ποιες είναι οι δυνάμεις και αδυναμίες σας;
       (Pee-es ee-nai ee dy-nah-mees ke ah-dy-nah-mee-es sas?)

554.   Describe your relevant experience.
       Περιγράψτε τη σχετική σας εμπειρία.
       (Peh-ree-grahp-ste tee scheh-tee-kee sas em-pee-ree-ah.)

555.   Why do you want to work here?
       Γιατί θέλετε να εργαστείτε εδώ;
       (Yah-tee the-leh-te nah er-gahs-tee-teh ed-oh?)

556.   Where do you see yourself in five years?
       Πού βλέπετε τον εαυτό σας σε πέντε χρόνια;
       (Poo vleh-peh-teh ton eh-af-to sas seh pen-deh hro-nee-ah?)

557.   How do you handle challenges at work?
       Πώς αντιμετωπίζετε τις προκλήσεις στη δουλειά;
       (Pos an-tee-me-toh-pee-zeh-teh tees pro-klee-sees stee dhoo-lee-ah?)

558.   What interests you about this position?
       Τι σας ενδιαφέρει για αυτή τη θέση;
       (Tee sas en-dee-ah-feh-ree yia af-tee tee the-see?)

559. Can you provide an example of your teamwork?
Μπορείτε να δώσετε ένα παράδειγμα της ομαδικής σας εργασίας;
(Bo-ree-teh nah tho-seh-teh eh-na pa-rah-deeg-ma tees oh-mah-dee-kees sas er-gah-see-as?)

560. What motivates you in your career?
Τι σας κινητοποιεί στην καριέρα σας;
(Tee sas kee-nee-toh-poy-ee stin kah-ree-eh-rah sas?)

561. Do you have any questions for us?
Έχετε κάποιες ερωτήσεις για εμάς;
(Eh-heh-teh kah-pee-es eh-roh-tee-sees yia eh-mas?)

562. Thank you for considering me for the role.
Ευχαριστώ που με λάβατε υπόψη για αυτόν τον ρόλο.
(Ef-hah-rees-toh poo meh lah-va-teh ee-pohp-see yia af-ton ton ro-lo.)

Office Communication

563. Send me an email about it.
Στείλτε μου ένα email γι' αυτό.
(Stee-lteh moo eh-na email yee af-to.)

564. Let's schedule a conference call.
Ας οργανώσουμε μια τηλεδιάσκεψη.
(As or-gah-no-soo-meh meeah tee-leh-thee-ah-skep-see.)

565. Could you clarify your message?
Μπορείτε να διευκρινίσετε το μήνυμά σας;
(Bo-ree-teh nah thee-ef-kree-nee-see-teh to mee-nee-mah sas?)

566.   I'll forward the document to you.
        Θα σας προωθήσω το έγγραφο.
        (*Tha sas pro-oh-thee-so to eng-grafo.*)

567.   Please reply to this message.
        Παρακαλώ απαντήστε σε αυτό το μήνυμα.
        (*Pa-ra-ka-lo a-pan-dee-ste se af-to to mee-nee-ma.*)

568.   We should have a team meeting.
        Πρέπει να έχουμε μια ομαδική συνάντηση.
        (*Pre-pee na eh-hoo-me mea oh-ma-dee-kee si-nan-tee-see.*)

        Idiomatic Expression: "Χάνω τα αυγά και τα καλάθια."
        Meaning: "Lose everything, a total failure."
        (Literal translation: "I lose the eggs and the baskets.")

569.   Check your inbox for updates.
        Ελέγξτε τον εισερχόμενο φάκελο σας για ενημερώσεις.
        (*Eh-len-xte ton ee-ser-ho-meno fa-kelo sas yia e-nee-me-ro-sees.*)

570.   I'll copy you on the correspondence.
        Θα σας κάνω αντίγραφο στην αλληλογραφία.
        (*Tha sas ka-no an-dee-gra-fo stin a-lee-lo-gra-fee-a.*)

571.   I'll send you the meeting agenda.
        Θα σας στείλω την ατζέντα της συνάντησης.
        (*Tha sas stee-lo tin a-jen-da tis si-nan-tee-sees.*)

572.   Use the internal messaging system.
        Χρησιμοποιήστε το εσωτερικό σύστημα μηνυμάτων.
        (*Hree-see-mo-pee-ee-ste to e-so-te-ri-ko see-stee-ma mee-nee-ma-ton.*)

573.   Keep everyone in the loop.
        Κρατήστε όλους ενημερωμένους για κάθε νέα εξέλιξη.
        (*Kra-tee-ste o-lous e-nee-me-ro-me-nous yia ka-the ne-a*
        ek-se-li-xi.)

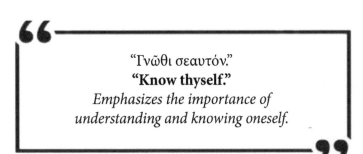

"Γνῶθι σεαυτόν."
"Know thyself."
Emphasizes the importance of
understanding and knowing oneself.

Cross Word Puzzle: Business & Work

(Provide the Greek translation for the following English words)

Across

5. - SERVICE
6. - PRODUCT
10. - WORK
11. - CONTRACT
13. - MARKETING
15. - BUSINESS

Down

1. - BOSS
2. - OFFICE
3. - CLIENT
4. - PROFESSIONAL
7. - TEAM
8. - PROJECT
9. - INCOME
12. - EMPLOYEE
14. - SALARY

Correct Answers:

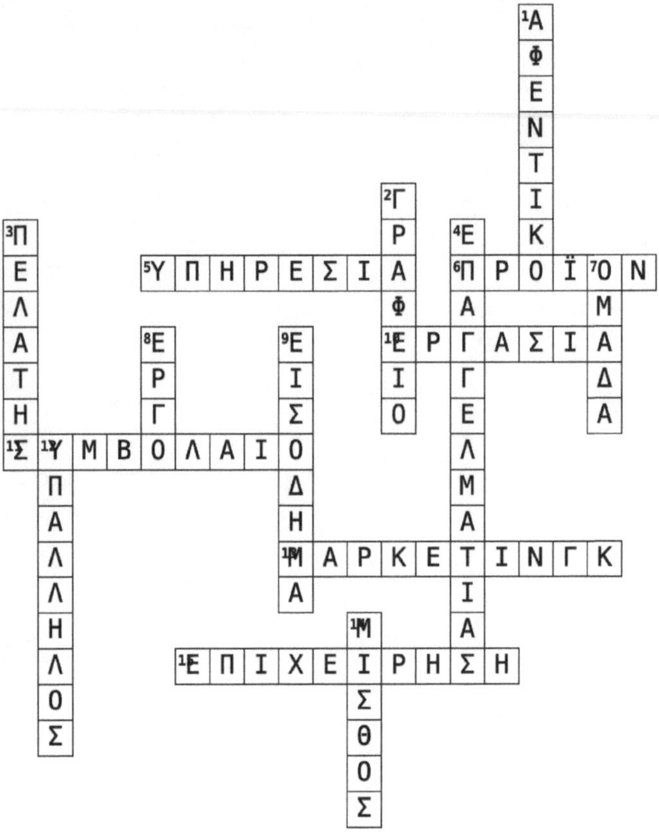

1 ΑΦΕΝΤΙΚΟ
2 ΓΡΑΦΕΙΟ
3 ΠΕΛΑΤΗΣ
4 ΕΠΑΓΓΕΛΜΑΤΙΑΣ
5 ΥΠΗΡΕΣΙΑ
6 ΠΡΟΪΟΝ
7 ΟΜΑΔΑ
8 ΕΡΓΟ
9 ΕΙΣΟΔΗΜΑ
10 ΕΡΓΑΣΙΑ
11 ΣΥΜΒΟΛΑΙΟ
12 ΥΠΑΛΛΗΛΟΣ
13 ΜΑΡΚΕΤΙΝΓΚ
14 ΜΙΣΘΟΣ
15 ΕΠΙΧΕΙΡΗΣΗ

EVENTS & ENTERTAINMENT

- BUYING TICKETS FOR CONCERTS, MOVIES OR EVENTS -
- DISCUSSING ENTERTAINMENT & LEISURE ACTIVITIES -
- EXPRESSING JOY OR DISAPPOINTMENT WITH AN EVENT -

Ticket Purchases

574. I'd like to buy two tickets for the concert.
Θα ήθελα να αγοράσω δύο εισιτήρια για τη συναυλία.
(Tha ee-the-la na a-go-ra-so dyo ee-si-ti-ria ya ti si-nav-li-a.)

575. Can I get tickets for the movie tonight?
Μπορώ να αγοράσω εισιτήρια για την αποψινή ταινία;
(Bo-ro na a-go-ra-so ee-si-ti-ria ya tin a-po-psi-ni te-ni-a?)

576. We need to book tickets for the upcoming event.
Χρειαζόμαστε να κλείσουμε εισιτήρια για την επερχόμενη εκδήλωση.
(Hree-a-zo-mas-te na kli-sou-me ee-si-ti-ria ya tin e-per-ho-me-ni ek-di-lo-si.)

577. What's the price of admission?
Ποια είναι η τιμή της εισόδου;
(Pia ee-nai ee ti-mi tis ee-so-dou?)

578. Do you offer any discounts for students?
Προσφέρετε κάποιες εκπτώσεις για φοιτητές;
(Pro-sfe-re-te ka-pi-es ekp-to-seis ya fi-ti-tes?)

579. Are there any available seats for the matinee?
Υπάρχουν διαθέσιμες θέσεις για τη ματινέ;
(Y-par-houn di-a-the-si-mes the-sis ya ti ma-ti-ne?)

580. How can I purchase tickets online?
Πώς μπορώ να αγοράσω εισιτήρια διαδικτυακά;
(Pos bo-ro na a-go-ra-so ee-si-ti-ria di-a-dik-ti-a-ka?)

581. Is there a box office nearby?
Υπάρχει κοντά ένα εκδοτήριο;
(*Y-par-hei kon-ta e-na ek-do-ti-rio?*)

582. Are tickets refundable if I can't attend?
Είναι επιστρέψιμα τα εισιτήρια αν δεν μπορώ να παρευρεθώ;
(*E-ne e-pi-stre-pi-ma ta ee-si-ti-ria an den bo-ro na pa-rev-re-tho?*)

583. Can I choose my seats for the show?
Μπορώ να επιλέξω τις θέσεις μου για την παράσταση;
(*Bo-ro na e-pi-le-xo tis the-sis mou ya tin pa-ras-ta-si?*)

584. Can I reserve tickets for the theater?
Μπορώ να κλείσω εισιτήρια για το θέατρο;
(*Bo-ro na kli-so ee-si-ti-ria ya to the-a-tro?*)

585. How early should I buy event tickets?
Πόσο νωρίς πρέπει να αγοράσω εισιτήρια για την εκδήλωση;
(*Po-so no-ris pre-pi na a-go-ra-so ee-si-ti-ria ya tin ek-di-lo-si?*)

586. Are there any VIP packages available?
Υπάρχουν διαθέσιμα VIP πακέτα;
(*Y-par-houn di-a-the-si-ma Vee-I-Pee pa-ke-ta?*)

587. What's the seating arrangement like?
Ποια είναι η διάταξη των θέσεων;
(*Pia ee-nai ee di-a-ta-xi ton the-seon?*)

> **Idiomatic Expression:** "Άνοιξε ο ουρανός." -
> Meaning: "It started pouring (raining heavily)."
> (Literal translation: "The sky opened.")

588. Is there a family discount for the movie?
Υπάρχει οικογενειακή έκπτωση για την ταινία;
(*I-pár-khi ee-ko-ye-nee-akí ék-pto-see yia tin té-nee-a?*)

589. I'd like to purchase tickets for my friends.
Θέλω να αγοράσω εισιτήρια για τους φίλους μου.
(*Thé-lo na a-go-rá-so ee-see-tí-ree-a yia toos fí-lous mou.*)

> **Fun Fact:** Greece celebrates its Independence Day on March 25th, coinciding with the Annunciation of the Virgin Mary.

590. Do they accept credit cards for tickets?
Δέχονται πιστωτικές κάρτες για εισιτήρια;
(*Dé-hon-te pee-sto-ti-kés kár-tes yia ee-see-tí-ree-a?*)

591. Are there any age restrictions for entry?
Υπάρχουν περιορισμοί ηλικίας για την είσοδο;
(*I-pár-houn pe-ri-o-ri-smí ee-li-kías yia tin í-so-do?*)

592. Can I exchange my ticket for a different date?
Μπορώ να αλλάξω το εισιτήριό μου για διαφορετική ημερομηνία;
(*Mbo-ró na a-lá-xo to ee-see-tí-ri-ó mou yia di-a-fo-re-ti-kí ee-me-ro-mee-nía?*)

Leisure Activities

593. What do you feel like doing this weekend?
Τι θέλετε να κάνετε αυτό το σαββατοκύριακο;
(*Ti thé-le-te na ká-ne-te af-tó to sav-va-to-kí-ri-a-ko?*)

94.　Let's discuss our entertainment options.
Ας συζητήσουμε τις επιλογές διασκέδασής μας.
(As si-zi-tí-sou-me tis e-pi-lo-gés di-as-ké-da-sís mas.)

> **Fun Fact:** Crete is the largest island in Greece and the fifth largest in the Mediterranean Sea.

95.　I'm planning a leisurely hike on Saturday.
Σχεδιάζω μια χαλαρή πεζοπορία το Σάββατο.
(Sche-diá-zo mia ha-la-rí pe-zo-po-rí-a to Sáv-va-to.)

96.　Do you enjoy outdoor activities like hiking?
Σας αρέσουν οι υπαίθριες δραστηριότητες όπως η πεζοπορία;
(Sas a-ré-soun ee i-pé-thries dras-ti-rió-ti-tes ó-pos ee pe-zo-po-rí-a?)

97.　Have you ever tried indoor rock climbing?
Έχετε ποτέ δοκιμάσει εσωτερική αναρρίχηση;
(É-he-te po-té do-ki-má-see e-so-te-ri-kí a-na-rí-chi-si?)

98.　I'd like to explore some new hobbies.
Θέλω να εξερευνήσω κάποια νέα χόμπι.
(Thé-lo na e-xe-re-fní-so ká-pia né-a hó-bi.)

99.　What are your favorite pastimes?
Ποια είναι τα αγαπημένα σας περάσματα του χρόνου;
(Pi-a í-ne ta a-ga-pi-mé-na sas pe-rás-ma-ta tou hró-nou?)

> **Cultural Insight:** 'Mati' or the evil eye is a superstitious belief. Blue eye-shaped amulets are common for warding off bad luck.

600. Are there any interesting events in town?
Υπάρχουν ενδιαφέροντα γεγονότα στην πόλη;
(*I-pár-houn en-di-a-fé-ron-ta ye-go-nó-ta stin pó-li?*)

601. Let's check out the local art exhibition.
Ας δούμε την τοπική τέχνη έκθεση.
(*As dóu-me tin to-pi-kí té-ch-ni ék-the-si.*)

602. How about attending a cooking class?
Τι λέτε για ένα μαγειρικό μάθημα;
(*Ti lé-te ya é-na ma-yei-ri-kó má-thi-ma?*)

603. Let's explore some new recreational activities.
Ας εξερευνήσουμε κάποιες νέες αναψυχτικές δραστηριότητες
(*As e-xe-re-fní-sou-me ká-pi-es né-es a-na-psych-ti-kés dras-ti-rió-ti-tes.*)

604. What's your go-to leisure pursuit?
Ποια είναι η αγαπημένη σας αναψυχή;
(*Pi-a í-ne i a-ga-pi-mé-ni sas a-na-psy-chí?*)

605. I'm considering trying a new hobby.
Σκέφτομαι να δοκιμάσω ένα νέο χόμπι.
(*Skéf-to-mai na do-ki-má-so é-na né-o hó-bi.*)

606. Have you ever attended a painting workshop?
Έχετε ποτέ παρακολουθήσει ένα εργαστήριο ζωγραφικής;
(*É-che-te po-té pa-ra-ko-lo-thí-sei é-na er-gas-tí-rio zo-gra-fi-kís?*)

> **Fun Fact:** Greece enjoys more than 250 days of
> sunshine—or 3,000 sunny hours—a year.

07.   What's your favorite way to unwind?
Ποιος είναι ο αγαπημένος σας τρόπος για χαλάρωση;
(*Pi-os í-ne o a-ga-pi-mé-nos sas tró-pos ya cha-lá-ro-si?*)

08.   I'm interested in joining a local club.
Ενδιαφέρομαι να εγγραφώ σε ένα τοπικό σύλλογο.
(*En-di-a-fé-ro-mai na eg-gra-fó se é-na to-pi-kó sí-llo-go.*)

09.   Let's plan a day filled with leisure.
Ας οργανώσουμε μια μέρα γεμάτη αναψυχή.
(*As or-ga-nó-sou-me mi-a mé-ra ye-má-ti a-na-psy-chí.*)

10.   Have you ever been to a live comedy show?
Έχετε ποτέ πάει σε ζωντανή κωμική παράσταση;
(*É-che-te po-té pá-i se zon-da-ní ko-mi-kí pa-rás-ta-si?*)

11.   I'd like to attend a cooking demonstration.
Θα ήθελα να παρακολουθήσω μια μαγειρική επίδειξη.
(*Tha í-the-la na pa-ra-ko-lo-thí-so mi-a ma-yei-ri-kí e-pí-dei-xi.*)

> **Fun Fact:** In Greek mythology, Mount Olympus was regarded as the "home of the gods."

Event Reactions

612.   That concert was amazing! I loved it!
Το συναυλία ήταν καταπληκτική! Μου άρεσε πολύ!
(*To sy-na-vli-a í-tan ka-ta-plek-ti-kí! Mou á-re-se po-lí!*)

613.   I had such a great time at the movie.
        Πέρασα τόσο υπέροχα στην ταινία.
        (Pé-rasa tó-so y-pé-ro-ha stin te-ne-ía.)

614.   The event exceeded my expectations.
        Η εκδήλωση ξεπέρασε τις προσδοκίες μου.
        (I ek-dí-lo-si xe-pé-ra-se tis pro-sdo-kí-es mou.)

615.   I was thrilled by the performance.
        Με ενθουσίασε η παράσταση.
        (Me en-thou-sí-a-se i pa-rás-ta-si.)

616.   It was an unforgettable experience.
        Ήταν μια αξέχαστη εμπειρία.
        (Í-tan mi-a a-xé-ha-sti em-pe-ri-ía.)

617.   I can't stop thinking about that show.
        Δεν μπορώ να σταματήσω να σκέφτομαι εκείνη την παράσταση.
        (Den mbo-ró na sta-ma-tí-so na skéf-to-mai e-kí-ni tin pa-rás-ta-si.)

618.   Unfortunately, the event was a letdown.
        Δυστυχώς, η εκδήλωση ήταν απογοητευτική.
        (Dys-ty-hós, i ek-dí-lo-si í-tan a-po-ghi-tef-ti-kí.)

619.   I was disappointed with the movie.
        Απογοητεύτηκα από την ταινία.
        (A-po-ghi-tef-tí-ka apó tin te-ne-ía.)

620.   The concert didn't meet my expectations.
        Η συναυλία δεν ικανοποίησε τις προσδοκίες μου.
        (I sy-na-vli-a den i-ka-no-pí-i-se tis pro-sdo-kí-es mou.)

621. I expected more from the exhibition.
Περίμενα περισσότερα από την έκθεση.
(Pe-rí-me-na pe-ris-só-te-ra apó tin ék-the-si.)

622. The event left me speechless; it was superb!
Το γεγονός με άφησε άφωνο· ήταν υπέροχο!
(To ye-go-nós me á-fi-se á-fo-no; í-tan y-pé-ro-ho!)

623. I was absolutely thrilled with the performance.
Ήμουν απόλυτα ενθουσιασμένος/η με την παράσταση.
(Í-moun a-pó-ly-ta en-thou-si-as-mé-nos/i me tin pa-rás-ta-si.)

624. The movie was a pleasant surprise.
Η ταινία ήταν μια ευχάριστη έκπληξη.
(I te-ne-ía í-tan mi-a ef-há-ris-ti ék-pli-xi.)

625. I had such a blast at the exhibition.
Διασκέδασα πολύ στην έκθεση.
(Dia-ské-da-sa po-lý stin ék-the-si.)

626. The concert was nothing short of fantastic.
Η συναυλία ήταν φανταστική.
(I sy-na-vli-a í-tan fan-ta-sti-kí.)

627. I'm still on cloud nine after the event.
Ακόμα βρίσκομαι στα επτά ουρανούς μετά το γεγονός.
(A-kó-ma vrí-sko-mai sta ep-tá ou-ra-noús me-tá to ye-go-nós.)

Travel Story: At a folklore museum in Ioannina, a guide described the artifacts as "Θησαυροί του χρόνου," or "Treasures of time," indicating their cultural value.

628.   I was quite underwhelmed by the show.
        Η παράσταση με απογοήτευσε αρκετά.
        (*I pa-rás-ta-si me a-po-goí-tef-se ar-ke-tá.*)

629.   I expected more from the movie.
        Περίμενα περισσότερα από την ταινία.
        (*Pe-rí-me-na pe-ris-só-te-ra apó tin te-ne-ía.*)

630.   Unfortunately, the exhibition didn't impress me.
        Δυστυχώς, η έκθεση δεν με εντυπωσίασε.
        (*Dys-ty-hós, i ék-the-si den me en-dy-po-sí-a-se.*)

"
"Η αγάπη ξεκινάει με ένα χαμόγελο."
"Love starts with a smile."
*The simplest gestures can lead to
deeper connections and feelings.*
"

Mini Lesson:
Basic Grammar Principles in Greek #2

Introduction:

In this continuation of our Greek grammar series, we delve deeper into the fascinating aspects of this ancient yet dynamic language. Building on the fundamentals, this lesson will broaden your understanding of Greek syntax, common expressions, and other intricate elements that enrich communication.

1. Sentence Structure:

Greek typically follows a Subject-Object-Verb (SOV) structure, though it can be flexible due to its rich inflectional system. This flexibility allows for emphasis on different parts of the sentence.

- Ο Πέτρος διαβάζει ένα βιβλίο. *(Peter is reading a book.)*
- Ένα βιβλίο διαβάζει ο Πέτρος. *(A book is being read by Peter.)*

2. The Subjunctive Mood:

The subjunctive in Greek is used to express wishes, hypotheses, or actions dependent on another action. It often follows particles like "να", "ας".

- Θέλω να πάω στη θάλασσα. *(I want to go to the sea.)*
- Ας πάμε στον κινηματογράφο. *(Let's go to the cinema.)*

3. Passive Voice:

Like the active voice, the passive voice in Greek has different tenses and is formed using specific verb endings.

- *Το σπίτι καθαρίζεται από τη Μαρία. (The house is cleaned by Maria.)*
- *Το γράμμα εστάλη. (The letter was sent.)*

4. Participle Forms:

Participles in Greek are verbal adjectives that express completed action or state and agree with nouns in gender, number, and case.

- *Ο γράφων άνθρωπος (The writing man)*
- *Τα ψημένα ψάρια (The cooked fish)*

5. Imperfective and Perfective Aspects:

Greek verbs have two aspects: imperfective (present, future, and past continuous) and perfective (simple past). These aspects indicate the nature of an action rather than its time.

- *Έτρεχα (I was running - imperfective)*
- *Έτρεξα (I ran - perfective)*

6. Use of Articles:

Greek uses definite and indefinite articles which agree in gender, number, and case with the noun they modify.

- *Ο κήπος (the garden)*
- *Ένας κήπος (a garden)*

Conclusion:

Understanding these aspects of Greek grammar will greatly enhance your ability to communicate and comprehend more complex Greek texts and dialogues. Practice regularly and immerse yourself in the language for the best results. Καλή τύχη! (Good luck!)

HEALTHCARE & MEDICAL NEEDS

- EXPLAINING SYMPTOMS TO A DOCTOR -
- REQUESTING MEDICAL ASSISTANCE -
- DISCUSSING MEDICATIONS AND TREATMENT -

Explaining Symptoms

631. I have a persistent headache.
      Έχω συνεχή πονοκέφαλο.
      (Eh-ho sy-ne-hí po-no-ké-fa-lo.)

632. My throat has been sore for a week.
      Έχω πονόλαιμο εδώ και μία εβδομάδα.
      (Eh-ho po-nó-le-mo e-dó ke mí-a ev-do-má-da.)

633. I've been experiencing stomach pain and nausea.
      Έχω πόνους στο στομάχι και ναυτία.
      (Eh-ho pó-nus sto sto-má-hi ke naf-tía.)

634. I have a high fever and chills.
      Έχω υψηλό πυρετό και ρίγη.
      (Eh-ho y-psi-ló py-re-tó ke rí-gi.)

635. My back has been hurting for a few days.
      Πονάει η πλάτη μου εδώ και μερικές μέρες.
      (Po-ná-i i plá-ti mou e-dó ke me-ri-kés mé-res.)

636. I'm coughing up yellow mucus.
      Βήχω και φτύνω κίτρινα φλέγματα.
      (Ví-ho ke fty-nó kí-tri-na flég-ma-ta.)

637. I have a rash on my arm.
      Έχω εξάνθημα στο χέρι μου.
      (Eh-ho ex-án-thi-ma sto hé-ri mou.)

> **Fun Fact:** The blue color on the Greek flag represents the sea and sky of Greece.

38. I've been having trouble breathing.
Έχω δυσκολία στην αναπνοή.
(Eh-ho dys-ko-lí-a stin a-na-pno-í.)

39. I feel dizzy and lightheaded.
Νιώθω ζάλη και λιποθυμία.
(Ni-ó-tho zá-li ke li-po-thy-mí-a.)

40. My joints are swollen and painful.
Έχω διογκωμένες και πονεμένες αρθρώσεις.
(Eh-ho di-o-go-mé-nes ke po-ne-mé-nes ar-thró-sis.)

41. I've had diarrhea for two days.
Έχω διάρροια εδώ και δύο μέρες.
(Eh-ho di-ár-ro-ia e-dó ke dýo mé-res.)

42. My eyes are red and itchy.
Τα μάτια μου είναι κόκκινα και φαγούρα.
(Ta má-tia mou eí-nai kók-ki-na ke fa-goú-ra.)

43. I've been vomiting since last night.
Έχω εμετούς από χθες βράδυ.
(Eh-ho e-me-tús a-pó hthes vrá-dy.)

44. I have a painful, persistent toothache.
Έχω έναν επίμονο και πονεμένο οδοντόπονο.
(Eh-ho é-nan e-pí-mo-no ke po-ne-mé-no o-don-tó-po-no.)

45. I'm experiencing fatigue and weakness.
Αισθάνομαι κούραση και αδυναμία.
(Ais-thá-no-mai kú-ra-si ke a-dy-na-mí-a.)

646. I've noticed blood in my urine.
Έχω παρατηρήσει αίμα στα ούρα μου.
(Eh-ho pa-ra-ti-rí-see é-ma sta oú-ra mou.)

647. My nose is congested, and I can't smell anything.
Έχω φραγμένη μύτη και δεν μπορώ να μυρίσω τίποτα.
(Eh-ho fra-ghmé-ni mí-ti ke den bo-ró na mi-rí-so tí-po-ta.)

648. I have a cut that's not healing properly.
Έχω μια πληγή που δεν επουλώνεται σωστά.
(Eh-ho mi-a pli-ghí pou den e-pou-ló-ne-tai so-stá.)

649. My ears have been hurting, and I can't hear well.
Με πονάνε τα αυτιά μου και δεν ακούω καλά.
(Me po-ná-ne ta af-ti-á mou ke den a-kó-o ka-lá.)

650. I think I might have a urinary tract infection.
Νομίζω ότι ίσως έχω μια λοίμωξη του ουροποιητικού.
(No-mí-zo ó-ti í-sos é-ho mi-a loí-mo-xi tou ou-ro-poi-i-ti-kóu.)

651. I've had trouble sleeping due to anxiety.
Έχω πρόβλημα με τον ύπνο λόγω άγχους.
(Eh-ho pró-vli-ma me ton íp-no ló-go án-hous.)

Requesting Medical Assistance

652. I need to see a doctor urgently.
Χρειάζομαι επειγόντως γιατρό.
(Hreiá-zo-mai e-pe-i-gón-tos yia-tró.)

53. Can you call an ambulance, please?
Μπορείτε να καλέσετε ασθενοφόρο, παρακαλώ;
(Bo-rí-te na ka-lé-se-te as-the-no-fó-ro, pa-ra-ka-ló?)

> **Travel Story:** In a Kalamata olive grove, a farmer said, "Κάθε ελιά έχει την ιστορία της," meaning "Every olive has its story," speaking of tradition and heritage.

54. I require immediate medical attention.
Χρειάζομαι άμεση ιατρική προσοχή.
(Hreiá-zo-mai á-me-si i-a-tri-kí pro-so-hí.)

55. Is there an available appointment today?
Υπάρχει διαθέσιμο ραντεβού σήμερα;
(I-pár-hi di-a-thé-si-mo ran-te-voú sí-me-ra?)

56. Please help me find a nearby clinic.
Παρακαλώ βοηθήστε με να βρω μια κοντινή κλινική.
(Pa-ra-ka-ló voi-thí-ste me na vro mi-a kon-ti-ní kli-ni-kí.)

57. I think I'm having a medical emergency.
Νομίζω ότι έχω μια ιατρική έκτακτη ανάγκη.
(No-mí-zo ó-ti é-ho mi-a i-a-tri-kí ék-tak-ti a-ná-gi.)

58. Can you recommend a specialist?
Μπορείτε να μου προτείνετε ειδικό;
(Bo-rí-te na mou pro-tí-ne-te i-di-kó?)

59. I'm in severe pain; can I see a doctor now?
Έχω έντονο πόνο; μπορώ να δω γιατρό τώρα;
(Eh-ho én-to-no pó-no; bo-ró na do yia-tró tó-ra?)

660. Is there a 24-hour pharmacy in the area?
Υπάρχει κάποιο φαρμακείο ανοιχτό 24 ώρες στην περιοχή;
(Ee-pár-khee ká-po-ee-o far-ma-kee-o a-nee-khtó éf-doh-mee-si o-res stin pe-ree-o-khí?)

661. I need a prescription refill.
Χρειάζομαι ανανέωση συνταγής.
(Khree-á-zo-mai a-na-née-o-see seen-ta-yís.)

662. Can you guide me to the nearest hospital?
Μπορείτε να με κατευθύνετε στο πλησιέστερο νοσοκομείο;
(Bo-rí-te na me ka-tef-thí-ne-te sto plee-see-és-te-ro no-so-ko-mee-o?)

663. I've cut myself and need medical assistance.
Έκοψα τον εαυτό μου και χρειάζομαι ιατρική βοήθεια.
(É-ko-psa ton e-af-tó mou ke khree-á-zo-mai ee-a-tri-kí vo-í-thee-a.)

664. My child has a high fever; what should I do?
Το παιδί μου έχει υψηλό πυρετό· τι πρέπει να κάνω;
(To pe-thee mou é-khee eep-see-ló pee-re-tó; tee pré-pee na ká-no?)

665. Is there a walk-in clinic nearby?
Υπάρχει κάποια κλινική χωρίς ραντεβού στην περιοχή;
(Ee-pár-khee ká-po-ee-a klee-nee-kée kho-rís ran-de-vou stin pe-ree-o-khí?)

666. I need medical advice about my condition.
Χρειάζομαι ιατρική συμβουλή για την κατάστασή μου.
(Khree-á-zo-mai ee-a-tri-kí seem-vou-lí ya tin ka-tás-ta-see mou.)

667. My medication has run out; I need a refill.
      **Τα φάρμακά μου τελείωσαν· χρειάζομαι
      επανασυνταγογράφηση.**
      (*Ta fár-ma-ká mou te-lee-ó-san; khree-á-zo-mai e-pa-na-seen-ta-
      go-grá-fee-see.*)

668. Can you direct me to an eye doctor?
      Μπορείτε να με κατευθύνετε σε οφθαλμίατρο;
      (*Bo-rí-te na me ka-tef-thí-ne-te se of-thal-mí-a-tro?*)

669. I've been bitten by a dog; I'm concerned.
      Δάγκωσε ένας σκύλος· ανησυχώ.
      (*Dág-ko-se é-nas skí-los; a-nee-see-khó.*)

670. Is there a dentist available for an emergency?
      Υπάρχει διαθέσιμος οδοντίατρος για έκτακτη περίπτωση;
      (*Ee-pár-khee thee-a-thé-see-mos o-don-tee-a-tros ya ék-tak-tee
      pe-ríp-to-see?*)

671. I think I might have food poisoning.
      Νομίζω ότι έχω δηλητηρίαση από φαγητό.
      (*No-mí-zo ó-ti é-kho dee-lee-tee-ree-á-see apó fa-yee-tó.*)

672. Can you help me find a pediatrician for my child?
      **Μπορείτε να με βοηθήσετε να βρω παιδίατρο για το παιδί
      μου;**
      (*Bo-rí-te na me vo-ee-thí-se-te na vro pe-thee-á-tro ya to pe-thee
      mou?*)

      Idiomatic Expression: "Γέμισε το ποτήρι." -
      Meaning: "That's the last straw."
      (Literal translation: "The glass filled up.")

Discussing Medications and Treatments

673.   What is this medication for?
Για τι χρησιμοποιείται αυτό το φάρμακο;
(Ya ti khree-see-mo-pee-é-tai af-tó to fár-ma-ko?)

674.   How often should I take this pill?
Πόσο συχνά πρέπει να παίρνω αυτό το χάπι;
(Pó-so sih-ná pré-pee na pé-rno af-tó to há-pi?)

675.   Are there any potential side effects?
Υπάρχουν πιθανές παρενέργειες;
(Ee-pár-houn pee-tha-nés pa-re-nér-yee-es?)

676.   Can I take this medicine with food?
Μπορώ να πάρω αυτό το φάρμακο με φαγητό;
(Bo-ró na pá-ro af-tó to fár-ma-ko me fa-yee-tó?)

677.   Should I avoid alcohol while on this medication?
Πρέπει να αποφεύγω το αλκοόλ ενώ παίρνω αυτό το φάρμακο;
(Pré-pee na a-po-fév-go to al-ko-ól e-nó pé-rno af-tó to fár-ma-ko?)

678.   Is it safe to drive while taking this?
Είναι ασφαλές να οδηγώ ενώ παίρνω αυτό το φάρμακο;
(Ee-ne as-fa-lés na o-dee-gó e-nó pé-rno af-tó to fár-ma-ko?)

679.   Are there any dietary restrictions?
Υπάρχουν διαιτητικοί περιορισμοί;
(Ee-pár-houn dee-ee-tee-ti-kí pe-ree-or-eez-mí?)

80. Can you explain the dosage instructions?
Μπορείτε να εξηγήσετε τις οδηγίες δοσολογίας;
(Bo-rí-te na ex-ee-yí-se-te tis o-dee-yí-es do-so-lo-yí-as?)

81. What should I do if I miss a dose?
Τι πρέπει να κάνω αν χάσω μία δόση;
(Ti pré-pee na ká-no an há-so mía dó-see?)

82. How long do I need to continue this treatment?
Για πόσο καιρό πρέπει να συνεχίσω αυτή τη θεραπεία;
(Ya pó-so ke-ró pré-pee na si-ne-hí-so af-tí ti the-ra-pee-á?)

83. Can I get a generic version of this medication?
Μπορώ να πάρω μια γενική έκδοση αυτού του φαρμάκου;
(Bo-ró na pá-ro mia ye-ni-kí ék-do-si af-toú tou far-má-kou?)

84. Is there a non-prescription alternative?
Υπάρχει εναλλακτική χωρίς συνταγή;
(Ee-pár-hi e-na-lak-ti-kí ho-rís sin-ta-yí?)

85. How should I store this medication?
Πώς πρέπει να αποθηκεύω αυτό το φάρμακο;
(Pós pré-pee na a-po-thi-kef-o af-tó to fár-ma-ko?)

86. Can you show me how to use this inhaler?
Μπορείτε να μου δείξετε πώς να χρησιμοποιώ αυτό τον εισπνευστήρα;
(Bo-rí-te na moo dí-xe-te pós na hree-see-mo-pee-ó af-tón ton ees-pnef-stí-ra?)

687. What's the expiry date of this medicine?
Ποια είναι η ημερομηνία λήξης αυτού του φαρμάκου;
(*Pia í-ne i i-me-ro-mi-nía lí-xis af-tú tu far-má-kou?*)

> **Fun Fact:** The famous Greek dance, Sirtaki, was popularized by the movie "Zorba the Greek."

688. Do I need to finish the entire course of antibiotics?
Πρέπει να ολοκληρώσω όλη τη θεραπεία με αντιβιοτικά;
(*Pré-pei na o-lo-kli-ró-so ó-li ti the-ra-pí-a me an-ti-vi-o-ti-ká?*)

689. Can I cut these pills in half?
Μπορώ να κόψω αυτά τα χάπια στη μέση;
(*Bo-ró na kóp-so af-tá ta há-pia sti mé-si?*)

690. Is there an over-the-counter pain reliever you recommend?
Προτείνετε κάποιο αναλγητικό χωρίς συνταγή;
(*Pro-tí-ne-te ká-pio a-nal-yi-ti-kó ho-rís sin-ta-ghí?*)

691. Can I take this medication while pregnant?
Μπορώ να πάρω αυτό το φάρμακο κατά τη διάρκεια της εγκυμοσύνης;
(*Bo-ró na pá-ro af-tó to fár-ma-ko ka-tá ti diár-keia tis eg-ki-mo-sí-nis?*)

692. What should I do if I experience an allergic reaction?
Τι πρέπει να κάνω αν παρουσιάσω αλλεργική αντίδραση;
(*Ti pré-pei na ká-no an pa-rou-siá-so a-le-rgi-kí an-dí-dra-si?*)

> **Fun Fact:** The name 'Greece' is not used by Greeks. They call their country 'Hellas' or 'Ellada.'

93.   Can you provide more information about this treatment plan?
      Μπορείτε να δώσετε περισσότερες πληροφορίες για αυτό το
      σχέδιο θεραπείας;
      (*Bo-rí-te na dó-se-te pe-ri-só-te-res pli-ro-fo-rí-es ya af-tó to*
      shé-di-o the-ra-pí-as?)

> "Η ζωή είναι σαν ποτάμι."
> **"Life is like a river."**
> *Life is ever-flowing and constantly changing.*

Word Search Puzzle: Healthcare

HOSPITAL
ΝΟΣΟΚΟΜΕΙΟ
DOCTOR
ΓΙΑΤΡΌΣ
MEDICINE
ΦΆΡΜΑΚΟ
PRESCRIPTION
ΣΥΝΤΑΓΉ
APPOINTMENT
ΡΑΝΤΕΒΟΎ
SURGERY
ΧΕΙΡΟΥΡΓΕΊΟ
VACCINE
ΕΜΒΌΛΙΟ
PHARMACY
ΦΑΡΜΑΚΕΊΟ
ILLNESS
ΑΣΘΈΝΕΙΑ
TREATMENT
ΘΕΡΑΠΕΊΑ
DIAGNOSIS
ΔΙΆΓΝΩΣΗ
RECOVERY
ΑΝΆΡΡΩΣΗ
SYMPTOM
ΣΎΜΠΤΩΜΑ
IMMUNIZATION
ΕΜΒΟΛΙΑΣΜΌΣ

```
I Y S Y N S R M G E V A Φ A N
F E Z O J K W O N B F M A N O
T X Q Z C A Z I T M B Z P A I
T B N O J P C T X C H Q M P T
X G W P E C Y W T I O J A P A
Y S Q X A Q N C B E S D K Ω Z
L W N V A I E N Έ Θ Σ A E Σ I
M Δ I A Γ N Ω Σ H H B B Ί H N
H U Q G N B R Y O B T J O U U
V I U P L X P S L K A N T M M
I R G Q L M P H R F U L Σ A M
Q D S D I I K V C H Q X Ό G I
O W N J T Ύ O B E T N A P S F
P R Y A T L R I I V D P T C W
Σ R L D V T L E Φ A P M A K O
Y J E R T L N S C S K A I A Ί
N V N S N I Y E I O P U Γ J E
T I C E C M P S M P V L W A Γ
A X S I P R O H O T V E U V P
Γ S D T B N I I A A A H R P Y
Ή E O B G D N P J R V E I Y O
M M G A L T Y K T E M P R R P
A S I F M B M R V I U A M T I
Ί D M E V M D L E H O M C G E
E Q N G W S E O A G L N O Y X
Π T E M B Ό Λ I O A R D O I R
A M Ω T Π M Y Σ O K E U Y O L
P E M B O Λ I A Σ M Ό Σ S H V
E O W F Q O I E M O K O Σ O N
Θ I U G U G P U W M A T R C I
```

158

Correct Answers:

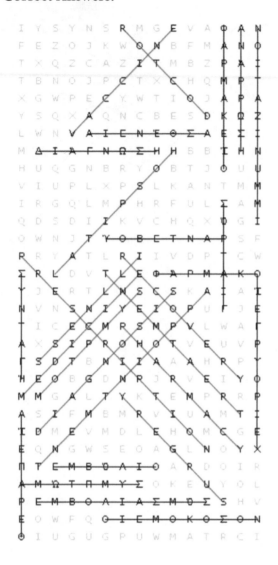

FAMILY & RELATIONSHIPS

- TALKING ABOUT FAMILY MEMBERS & RELATIONSHIPS -
- DISCUSSING PERSONAL LIFE & EXPERIENCES -
- EXPRESSING EMOTIONS & SENTIMENTS -

Family Members and Relationships

694. He's my younger brother.
Είναι ο νεότερος αδελφός μου.
(Eí-nai o neó-te-ros a-del-fós mou.)

695. She's my cousin from my mother's side.
Είναι η ξαδέλφη μου από τη μητρική πλευρά.
(Eí-nai i xa-dél-fi mou apó ti mi-tri-kí pleu-rá.)

696. My grandparents have been married for 50 years.
Οι παππούδες μου είναι παντρεμένοι εδώ και πενήντα χρόνια
(I pa-pou-des mou eí-nai pan-tre-mé-noi e-dó kai pe-nín-ta chro-ni-a.)

697. We're like sisters from another mister.
Είμαστε σαν αδελφές από διαφορετικό πατέρα.
(Eí-ma-ste san a-del-fés apó di-a-fo-re-ti-kó pa-té-ra.)

698. He's my husband's best friend.
Είναι ο καλύτερος φίλος του συζύγου μου.
(Eí-nai o ka-lý-te-ros fí-los tou sy-zy-gou mou.)

699. She's my niece on my father's side.
Είναι η ανιψιά μου από πατρική πλευρά.
(Eí-nai i a-nip-si-á mou apó pa-tri-kí pleu-rá.)

700. They are my in-laws.
Είναι οι πεθεροί μου.
(Eí-nai i pe-the-roí mou.)

01. Our family is quite close-knit.
Η οικογένειά μας είναι πολύ συνδεδεμένη.
(*I oi-ko-gé-nei-a mas eí-nai po-lý syn-de-de-mé-ni.*)

02. He's my adopted son.
Είναι ο υιοθετημένος γιος μου.
(*Eí-nai o yi-o-the-ti-mé-nos yios mou.*)

03. She's my half-sister.
Είναι η μισή μου αδελφή.
(*Eí-nai i mi-sí mou a-del-fí.*)

> **Travel Story:** While tasting baklava in a Thessaloniki bakery, the baker remarked, "Η γλύκα φέρνει χαρά," translating to "Sweetness brings joy."

04. My parents are divorced.
Οι γονείς μου είναι διαζευγμένοι.
(*I go-nís mou eí-nai di-a-zev-gmé-noi.*)

05. He's my fiancé.
Είναι ο αρραβωνιαστικός μου.
(*Eí-nai o a-rav-o-ni-as-ti-kós mou.*)

06. She's my daughter-in-law.
Είναι η νύφη μου.
(*Eí-nai i ný-fi mou.*)

> **Idiomatic Expression:** "Είμαι στα κάγκελα." -
> Meaning: "I'm on edge or very anxious."
> (Literal translation: "I am on the railings.")

707.   We're childhood friends.
        Είμαστε φίλοι από παιδική ηλικία.
        (Eí-ma-ste fí-loi apó pe-di-kí i-li-kí-a.)

708.   My twin brother and I are very close.
        Εγώ και ο δίδυμος αδελφός μου είμαστε πολύ κοντά.
        (Egó kai o dí-dy-mos a-del-fós mou eí-ma-ste po-lý kon-tá.)

709.   He's my godfather.
        Είναι ο νονός μου.
        (Eí-nai o no-nós mou.)

710.   She's my stepsister.
        Είναι η θετή μου αδελφή.
        (Eí-nai i the-tí mou a-del-fí.)

711.   My aunt is a world traveler.
        Η θεία μου είναι παγκόσμια ταξιδεύτρια.
        (I thi-a mou eí-nai pag-kó-smia tax-i-deú-tria.)

712.   We're distant relatives.
        Είμαστε μακρινοί συγγενείς.
        (Eí-ma-ste mak-ri-noí syn-gen-eís.)

713.   He's my brother-in-law.
        Είναι ο γαμπρός μου.
        (Eí-nai o gam-prós mou.)

714.   She's my ex-girlfriend.
        Είναι η πρώην κοπέλα μου.
        (Eí-nai i pró-in ko-pé-la mou.)

Personal Life and Experiences

715.   I've traveled to over 20 countries.
       Έχω ταξιδέψει σε πάνω από είκοσι χώρες.
       (É-cho ta-xi-dép-sei se pá-no apó eí-ko-si chó-res.)

716.   She's an avid hiker and backpacker.
       Είναι παθιασμένη πεζοπόρος και ταξιδεύτρια με σακίδιο.
       (Eí-nai pa-thi-a-smé-ni pe-zo-pó-ros kai ta-xi-deú-tria me sa-kí-di-o.)

717.   I enjoy cooking and trying new recipes.
       Μου αρέσει να μαγειρεύω και να δοκιμάζω νέες συνταγές.
       (Mou a-ré-sei na ma-yei-ré-vo kai na do-ki-má-zo né-es syn-ta-gés.)

718.   He's a professional photographer.
       Είναι επαγγελματίας φωτογράφος.
       (Eí-nai e-pa-gel-ma-tí-as fo-to-grá-fos.)

719.   I'm passionate about environmental conservation.
       Έχω πάθος για την προστασία του περιβάλλοντος.
       (É-cho pá-thos gia tin pro-sta-sía tou pe-ri-vál-lon-tos.)

720.   She's a proud dog owner.
       Είναι περήφανη ιδιοκτήτρια σκύλου.
       (Eí-nai pe-rí-fa-ni i-di-ok-tí-tria ský-lou.)

721.   I love attending live music concerts.
       Αγαπώ να παρακολουθώ συναυλίες ζωντανής μουσικής.
       (A-ga-pó na pa-ra-ko-lou-thó sy-na-vli-és zon-da-nís mou-si-kís.)

722. He's an entrepreneur running his own business.
Είναι επιχειρηματίας που διευθύνει τη δική του επιχείρηση.
(*Eí-nai e-pi-chei-ri-ma-tí-as pou di-e-fthí-nei ti di-kí tou e-pi-chí-ri-si.*)

723. I've completed a marathon.
Έχω τελειώσει έναν μαραθώνιο.
(*É-cho te-lió-si é-nan ma-ra-thó-nio.*)

724. She's a dedicated volunteer at a local shelter.
Είναι αφοσιωμένη εθελόντρια σε τοπικό καταφύγιο.
(*Eí-nai a-fo-sio-mé-ni e-the-lón-tria se to-pi-kó ka-ta-fí-gio.*)

725. I'm a history buff.
Είμαι λάτρης της ιστορίας.
(*Eí-mai lá-tris tis is-to-rí-as.*)

726. I'm a proud parent of three children.
Είμαι περήφανος γονιός τριών παιδιών.
(*Eí-mai pe-rí-fa-nos go-niós trión pe-di-ón.*)

727. I've recently taken up painting.
Πρόσφατα άρχισα να ζωγραφίζω.
(*Pró-sfa-ta ár-chi-sa na zo-gra-fí-zo.*)

728. She's a film enthusiast.
Είναι λάτρης των ταινιών.
(*Eí-nai lá-tris ton te-ni-ón.*)

729. I enjoy gardening in my free time.
Απολαμβάνω την κηπουρική στον ελεύθερο χρόνο μου.
(*A-po-lam-vá-no tin ki-pou-ri-kí ston e-léf-the-ro chró-no mou.*)

30. He's an astronomy enthusiast.
Είναι λάτρης της αστρονομίας.
(*Eí-nai lá-tris tis as-tro-no-mi-as.*)

31. I've skydived twice.
Έχω κάνει ελεύθερη πτώση δύο φορές.
(*É-cho ká-nei e-lef-the-ri ptó-si dýo fo-rés.*)

32. She's a fitness trainer.
Είναι γυμνάστρια φυσικής κατάστασης.
(*Eí-nai gym-nás-tria fy-si-kís ka-tás-ta-sis.*)

33. I love collecting vintage records.
Λατρεύω να συλλέγω βιντάζ δίσκους.
(*La-treú-o na sy-lé-go vin-táz dí-skous.*)

34. He's an experienced scuba diver.
Είναι έμπειρος δύτης.
(*Eí-nai ém-pi-ros dý-tis.*)

35. He's a bookworm and a literature lover.
Είναι βιβλιοφάγος και λάτρης της λογοτεχνίας.
(*Eí-nai vi-vli-o-fá-gos kai lá-tris tis lo-go-te-chi-ní-as.*)

> **Fun Fact:** Kalamata, a city in Greece, is famous for its
> unique and flavorful black olives.

Expressing Emotions and Sentiments

36. I feel overjoyed on my birthday.
Νιώθω πολύ χαρούμενος/η την ημέρα των γενεθλίων μου.
(*Nió-tho po-lý cha-roú-me-nos/i tin i-mé-ra ton
ge-ne-thli-on mou.*)

737. She's going through a tough time right now.
Περνάει μια δύσκολη περίοδο αυτή τη στιγμή.
(*Per-na-ee mia dí-sko-li pe-río-do af-tí ti stig-mí.*)

738. I'm thrilled about my upcoming vacation.
Είμαι ενθουσιασμένος για τις επερχόμενες διακοπές μου.
(*Eí-mai en-thou-sia-smé-nos gia tis e-per-chó-me-nes di-a-ko-pés mou.*)

739. He's heartbroken after the breakup.
Είναι συντετριμμένος μετά τον χωρισμό.
(*Eí-nai syn-te-trim-mé-nos me-tá ton cho-ris-mó.*)

740. I'm absolutely ecstatic about the news.
Είμαι απόλυτα ενθουσιασμένος για τα νέα.
(*Eí-mai a-pó-ly-ta en-thou-sia-smé-nos gia ta né-a.*)

741. She's feeling anxious before the big presentation.
Αισθάνεται αγχωμένη πριν τη μεγάλη παρουσίαση.
(*Ais-thá-ne-tai ang-cho-mé-ni prin ti me-gá-li pa-rou-siá-si.*)

742. I'm proud of my team's achievements.
Είμαι περήφανος για τις επιτυχίες της ομάδας μου.
(*Eí-mai pe-rí-fa-nos gia tis e-pi-ty-chí-es tis o-má-das mou.*)

743. He's devastated by the loss.
Είναι καταρρακωμένος από την απώλεια.
(*Eí-nai ka-tar-ra-ko-mé-nos apó tin apó-leia.*)

44. I'm grateful for the support I received.
Είμαι ευγνώμων για την υποστήριξη που έλαβα.
(*Eí-mai ev-gnó-mon gia tin y-po-stí-ri-xi pou é-la-va.*)

45. She's experiencing a mix of emotions.
Βιώνει ένα μείγμα συναισθημάτων.
(*Vió-nei é-na míg-ma syn-ai-sthi-má-ton.*)

46. I'm content with where I am in life.
Είμαι ικανοποιημένος με τη θέση μου στη ζωή.
(*Eí-mai i-ka-no-poi-i-mé-nos me ti thé-si mou sti zo-í.*)

47. He's overwhelmed by the workload.
Είναι πλημμυρισμένος από το φόρτο εργασίας.
(*Eí-nai plim-mi-ris-mé-nos apó to fór-to er-ga-sí-as.*)

48. I'm in awe of the natural beauty here.
Είμαι έκπληκτος από τη φυσική ομορφιά εδώ.
(*Eí-mai ék-plik-tos apó ti fy-si-kí o-mor-fiá e-dó.*)

> **Language Learning Tip:** Write in Greek Daily - Keep a journal where you write a few sentences in Greek every day.

49. She's relieved the exams are finally over.
Είναι ανακουφισμένη που τελείωσαν επιτέλους οι εξετάσεις.
(*Eí-nai a-na-kou-fi-sme-ni pou te-lí-o-san e-pi-té-lous oi e-xe-tá-seis.*)

750. I'm excited about the new job opportunity.
Είμαι ενθουσιασμένος για τη νέα ευκαιρία εργασίας.
(*Eí-mai en-thou-sia-smé-nos gia ti né-a ef-kai-rí-a er-ga-sí-as.*)

Travel Story: At the ancient theater of Epidaurus, a visitor whispered, "Οι πέτρες μιλάνε," meaning "The stones speak," alluding to the site's historical echoes.

751. I'm nostalgic about my childhood.
Νοσταλγώ τα παιδικά μου χρόνια.
(Nos-tal-gó ta pe-di-ká mou chró-nia.)

752. She's confused about her future.
Είναι μπερδεμένη για το μέλλον της.
(Eí-nai ber-de-mé-ni gia to mél-lon tis.)

753. I'm touched by the kindness of strangers.
Είμαι συγκινημένος από την καλοσύνη αγνώστων.
(Eí-mai sy-gki-ni-mé-nos apó tin ka-lo-sý-ni ag-nó-ston.)

754. He's envious of his friend's success.
Ζηλεύει την επιτυχία του φίλου του.
(Zi-leú-ei tin e-pi-ty-chí-a tou fí-lou tou.)

755. I'm hopeful for a better tomorrow.
Ελπίζω σε ένα καλύτερο αύριο.
(El-pí-zo se é-na ka-lý-te-ro á-vri-o.)

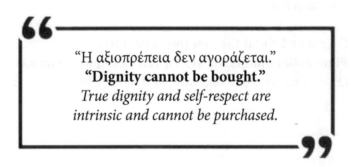

"Η αξιοπρέπεια δεν αγοράζεται."
"Dignity cannot be bought."
True dignity and self-respect are intrinsic and cannot be purchased.

Interactive Challenge: Family & Relationships
(Link each English word with their corresponding meaning in Greek)

1) Family   Φιλία

2) Parents   Σύζυγος

3) Siblings   Παιδιά

4) Children   Διαζύγιο

5) Grandparents   Γάμος

6) Spouse   Συγγενείς

7) Marriage   Παππούδες και γιαγιάδες

8) Love   Αγάπη

9) Friendship   Υιοθεσία

10) Relatives   Οικογένεια

11) In-laws   Αδέλφια

12) Divorce   Συγγενείς από το γάμο

13) Adoption   Γονείς

14) Cousins   Ανιψιά

15) Niece   Ξαδέλφια

Correct Answers:

1. Family - Οικογένεια
2. Parents - Γονείς
3. Siblings - Αδέλφια
4. Children - Παιδιά
5. Grandparents - Παππούδες και γιαγιάδες
6. Spouse - Σύζυγος
7. Marriage - Γάμος
8. Love - Αγάπη
9. Friendship - Φιλία
10. Relatives - Συγγενείς
11. In-laws - Συγγενείς από το γάμο
12. Divorce - Διαζύγιο
13. Adoption - Υιοθεσία
14. Cousins - Ξαδέλφια
15. Niece - Ανιψιά

TECHNOLOGY & COMMUNICATION

- USING TECHNOLOGY-RELATED PHRASES -
- INTERNET ACCESS AND COMMUNICATION TOOLS -
- TROUBLESHOOTING TECHNICAL ISSUES -

Using Technology

756.   I use my smartphone for various tasks.
       Χρησιμοποιώ το smartphone μου για διάφορες εργασίες.
       (Chree-see-mo-poi-ó to smartphone mou gia diá-fo-res er-ga-sí-es.)

757.   The computer is an essential tool in my work.
       Ο υπολογιστής είναι απαραίτητο εργαλείο στη δουλειά μου.
       (O ypo-lo-gi-stís eí-nai a-pa-raí-ti-to er-ga-lí-o sti dou-lei-á mou.

758.   I'm learning how to code and develop software.
       Μαθαίνω πώς να προγραμματίζω και να αναπτύσσω λογισμικό.
       (Ma-thé-no pós na pro-gram-ma-tí-zo kai na a-nap-týs-so lo-gis-mi-kó.)

759.   My tablet helps me stay organized.
       Το tablet μου με βοηθά να παραμένω οργανωμένος.
       (To tablet mou me voi-thá na pa-ra-mé-no or-ga-no-mé-nos.)

760.   I enjoy exploring new apps and software.
       Μου αρέσει να εξερευνώ νέες εφαρμογές και λογισμικό.
       (Mou a-ré-sei na e-xe-rev-nó né-es e-far-mo-gés kai lo-gis-mi-kó.

       Fun Fact: Many scientific terms in English and other
       languages are derived from Greek.

761.   Smartwatches are becoming more popular.
       Τα έξυπνα ρολόγια γίνονται όλο και πιο δημοφιλή.
       (Ta éx-y-pna ro-ló-gia gí-non-tai ó-lo kai pio di-mo-fi-lí.)

62. Virtual reality technology is fascinating.
Η τεχνολογία της εικονικής πραγματικότητας είναι συναρπαστική.
(*I teh-no-lo-gí-a tis ei-ko-ni-kís prag-ma-ti-kó-ti-tas eí-nai sy-nar-pas-ti-kí.*)

63. Artificial intelligence is changing industries.
Η τεχνητή νοημοσύνη αλλάζει τις βιομηχανίες.
(*I teh-ni-tí no-i-mo-sý-ni al-lá-zei tis vi-o-mi-cha-ní-es.*)

64. I like to customize my gadgets.
Μου αρέσει να προσαρμόζω τις συσκευές μου.
(*Mou a-ré-sei na pro-sar-mó-zo tis sys-kev-és mou.*)

65. E-books have replaced physical books for me.
Τα ηλεκτρονικά βιβλία έχουν αντικαταστήσει τα φυσικά βιβλία για εμένα.
(*Ta i-lek-tro-ni-ká vi-vlí-a é-choun an-ti-ka-ta-stí-sei ta fy-si-ká vi-vlí-a gia e-mé-na.*)

66. Social media platforms connect people worldwide.
Οι πλατφόρμες κοινωνικών δικτύων συνδέουν ανθρώπους παγκοσμίως.
(*Oi plat-fór-mes ki-no-ni-kón dik-tyón syn-dé-oun an-thró-pous pa-go-smi-ós.*)

67. I'm a fan of wearable technology.
Είμαι φαν της φορετής τεχνολογίας.
(*Eí-mai fan tis fo-re-tís teh-no-lo-gí-as.*)

68. The latest gadgets always catch my eye.
Τα τελευταία gadgets πάντα τραβούν το βλέμμα μου.
(*Ta te-lef-ta-ía gadgets pán-ta tra-vún to vlém-ma mou.*)

769. My digital camera captures high-quality photos.
Η ψηφιακή μου κάμερα τραβάει φωτογραφίες υψηλής ποιότητας.
(*I psi-fi-a-kí mou ká-me-ra tra-vá-ei fo-to-gra-fí-es yp-sí-lis pi-ó-ti-tas.*)

770. Home automation simplifies daily tasks.
Η αυτοματοποίηση στο σπίτι απλοποιεί τις καθημερινές εργασίες.
(*I af-to-ma-to-po-í-i-si sto spí-ti ap-lo-po-ií tis ka-thi-me-ri-nés er-ga-sí-es.*)

771. I'm into 3D printing as a hobby.
Με ενδιαφέρει ως χόμπι η 3D εκτύπωση.
(*Me en-di-a-fé-rei os chó-bi i 3D ek-tý-po-si.*)

772. Streaming services have revolutionized entertainment.
Οι υπηρεσίες streaming έχουν επαναστατήσει την ψυχαγωγία
(*I i-pe-re-sí-es streaming é-choun e-pa-na-sta-tí-si tin psy-cha-go-gí-a.*)

773. The Internet of Things (IoT) is expanding.
Το Διαδίκτυο των Πραγμάτων (IoT) επεκτείνεται.
(*To Di-a-dík-tyo ton Prag-má-ton (IoT) e-pek-teí-ne-tai.*)

774. I'm into gaming, both console and PC.
Μου αρέσουν τα βιντεοπαιχνίδια, και σε κονσόλα και σε υπολογιστή.
(*Mou a-ré-soun ta vin-te-o-pa-ich-ní-di-a, kai se kon-só-la kai se y-po-lo-gi-stí.*)

775. Wireless headphones make life more convenient.
Τα ασύρματα ακουστικά καθιστούν τη ζωή πιο βολική.
(*Ta a-sýr-ma-ta a-kous-ti-ká ka-thís-toun ti zo-í pi-o vo-li-kí.*)

776. Cloud storage is essential for my work.
Η αποθήκευση στο νέφος είναι απαραίτητη για τη δουλειά μου.
(*I a-po-thí-kef-si sto né-fos eí-nai a-pa-rái-ti-ti gia ti dou-lei-á mou.*)

> **Travel Story:** On the streets of Chania, a local mentioned, "Κάθε γωνιά κρύβει μια ιστορία," which translates to "Every corner hides a story," illustrating the city's rich past.

Internet Access and Communication Tools

777. I rely on high-speed internet for work.
Βασίζομαι στο γρήγορο διαδίκτυο για τη δουλειά μου.
(*Va-sí-zo-mai sto grí-goro di-a-dík-tyo gia ti dou-lei-á mou.*)

778. Video conferencing is crucial for remote meetings.
Η τηλεδιάσκεψη είναι κρίσιμη για απομακρυσμένες συναντήσεις.
(*I ti-le-diá-skep-si eí-nai kri-si-mi gia a-po-ma-krys-mé-nes sy-nan-tí-seis.*)

779. Social media helps me stay connected with friends.
Τα κοινωνικά δίκτυα με βοηθούν να παραμένω σε επαφή με τους φίλους μου.
(*Ta ki-no-ni-ká dík-tya me voi-thoún na pa-ra-mé-no se e-pa-fí me tous fí-lous mou.*)

780. Email is my primary mode of communication.
Το email είναι ο κύριος τρόπος επικοινωνίας μου.
(*To email eí-nai o kí-rios tró-pos e-pi-ko-i-no-ní-as mou.*)

781. I use messaging apps to chat with family.
Χρησιμοποιώ εφαρμογές μηνυμάτων για να συνομιλώ με την οικογένειά μου.
(Chri-si-mo-poi-ó ef-ar-mo-gés mi-ny-má-ton gia na si-no-mi-ló me tin oi-ko-gé-ni-a mou.)

782. Voice and video calls keep me in touch with loved ones.
Οι φωνητικές και βιντεοκλήσεις με κρατούν σε επαφή με τους αγαπημένους μου.
(I fo-ni-ti-kés kai vin-de-o-klí-seis me kra-tún se e-pa-fí me tous a-ga-pi-mé-nous mou.)

783. Online forums are a great source of information.
Τα διαδικτυακά φόρουμ είναι μια εξαιρετική πηγή πληροφοριών.
(Ta di-a-dik-tya-ká fó-rum eí-nai mi-a ex-er-e-ti-kí pi-gí pli-ro-fo-ri-ón.)

784. I trust encrypted messaging services for privacy.
Εμπιστεύομαι τις κρυπτογραφημένες υπηρεσίες μηνυμάτων για την ιδιωτικότητα.
(Em-pis-tév-o-mai tis krip-to-gra-fi-mé-nes i-pe-re-sí-es mi-ny-má-ton gia tin i-di-o-ti-kó-ti-ta.)

785. Webinars are a valuable resource for learning.
Τα διαδικτυακά σεμινάρια είναι πολύτιμος πόρος για μάθηση.
(Ta di-a-dik-tya-ká se-mi-ná-ria eí-nai po-lý-ti-mos pó-ros gia má-thi-si.)

786. VPNs enhance online security and privacy.
Τα VPN βελτιώνουν την ασφάλεια και την ιδιωτικότητα στο διαδίκτυο.
(Ta VPN ve-li-ó-noun tin as-fá-lei-a kai tin i-di-o-ti-kó-ti-ta sto di-a-dík-tyo.)

87. Cloud-based collaboration tools are essential for teamwork.
Τα εργαλεία συνεργασίας βασισμένα στο νέφος είναι απαραίτητα για την ομαδική εργασία.
(*Ta er-ga-leí-a si-ne-r-ga-sí-as va-sis-mé-na sto né-fos eí-nai a-pa-rái-ti-ta gia tin o-ma-di-kí er-ga-sí-a.*)

88. I prefer using a wireless router at home.
Προτιμώ τη χρήση ασύρματου δρομολογητή στο σπίτι.
(*Pro-ti-mó ti chrí-si a-sýr-ma-tou dro-mo-lo-gi-tí sto spí-ti.*)

89. Online banking simplifies financial transactions.
Η διαδικτυακή τραπεζική απλοποιεί τις χρηματοοικονομικές συναλλαγές.
(*I di-a-dik-tya-kí tra-pe-zi-kí ap-lo-poi-eí tis chri-ma-too-i-ko-no-mi-kés si-nal-la-gés.*)

> **Fun Fact:** Ancient Greek theater, which began as part of religious festivals, is the root of Western theatrical tradition.

90. VoIP services are cost-effective for international calls.
Οι υπηρεσίες VoIP είναι οικονομικές για διεθνείς κλήσεις.
(*I i-pe-re-sí-es VoIP eí-nai i-ko-no-mi-kés gia di-eth-nís klí-seis.*)

91. I enjoy online shopping for convenience.
Απολαμβάνω τις διαδικτυακές αγορές για την ευκολία.
(*A-po-lam-vá-no tis di-a-dik-tya-kés a-go-rés gia tin ef-ko-lí-a.*)

92. Social networking sites connect people globally.
Οι κοινωνικές δικτυακές πλατφόρμες συνδέουν τους ανθρώπους παγκοσμίως.
(*I ki-no-ni-kés dik-tya-kés plat-fór-mes sin-dé-oun tous an-thró-pous pa-go-smi-ós.*)

793. E-commerce platforms offer a wide variety of products.
Οι πλατφόρμες ηλεκτρονικού εμπορίου προσφέρουν μια
ευρεία ποικιλία προϊόντων.
(*I pla-tfór-mes i-lek-tron-i-kú em-porí-ou pro-sfé-roun mi-a
ev-ri-a pi-ki-lí-a pro-í-on-ton.*)

> **Idiomatic Expression:** "Έχω τον κόσμο μου." -
> Meaning: "I have my own problems."
> (Literal translation: "I have my world.")

794. Mobile banking apps make managing finances easy.
Οι εφαρμογές κινητής τραπεζικής διευκολύνουν τη διαχείρισι
των οικονομικών.
(*I ef-ar-mo-gés ki-ni-tís tra-pe-zi-kís di-ef-ko-lí-noun ti di-a-hí-r
si ton oi-ko-no-mi-kón.*)

795. I'm active on professional networking sites.
Είμαι ενεργός σε διαδικτυακές πλατφόρμες επαγγελματικής
δικτύωσης.
(*Eí-mai e-ner-gós se di-a-dik-tya-kés pla-tfór-mes
e-pa-gel-ma-ti-kís dik-tí-o-sis.*)

796. Virtual private networks protect my online identity.
Τα εικονικά ιδιωτικά δίκτυα προστατεύουν την διαδικτυακή
μου ταυτότητα.
(*Ta i-ko-ni-ká i-di-o-ti-ká dík-tya pro-sta-te-voún tin
di-a-dik-tya-kí mou taf-tó-ti-ta.*)

797. Instant messaging apps are great for quick chats.
Οι εφαρμογές άμεσης ανταλλαγής μηνυμάτων είναι ιδανικές
για γρήγορες συνομιλίες.
(*I ef-ar-mo-gés á-mesis an-ta-la-gís mi-ny-má-ton eí-nai
i-da-ni-kés gia grí-gores si-no-mi-lí-es.*)

Troubleshooting Technical Issues

98. My computer is running slow; I need to fix it.
   Ο υπολογιστής μου λειτουργεί αργά; πρέπει να τον επιδιορθώσω.
   (O i-po-lo-gis-tís mou lei-tour-gí ar-gá; pré-pi na ton e-pi-di-or-thó-so.)

99. I'm experiencing network connectivity problems.
   Αντιμετωπίζω προβλήματα συνδεσιμότητας δικτύου.
   (An-ti-me-to-pí-zo pro-vlí-ma-ta sin-de-si-mó-ti-tas dik-tí-ou.)

00. The printer isn't responding to my print commands.
   Ο εκτυπωτής δεν ανταποκρίνεται στις εντολές εκτύπωσής μου.
   (O ek-ti-po-tís den an-ta-po-krí-ne-tai stis en-to-lés ek-tí-po-sís mou.)

   Fun Fact: Cats are a common and beloved sight throughout Greece and are considered natural pest controllers.

01. My smartphone keeps freezing; it's frustrating.
   Το κινητό μου συνεχώς κολλάει· είναι απογοητευτικό.
   (To ki-ni-tó mou si-ne-hós ko-lá-i; eí-nai a-po-go-i-tef-ti-kó.)

02. The Wi-Fi signal in my house is weak.
   Το σήμα Wi-Fi στο σπίτι μου είναι αδύναμο.
   (To sí-ma Wi-Fi sto spí-ti mou eí-nai a-dí-na-mo.)

03. I can't access certain websites; it's a concern.
   Δεν μπορώ να αποκτήσω πρόσβαση σε ορισμένες ιστοσελίδες· αυτό είναι ανησυχητικό.
   (Den bo-ró na a-po-ktí-so pró-sva-si se o-ris-mé-nes is-to-se-lí-des; af-tó eí-nai a-ni-si-hi-ti-kó.)

804. My laptop battery drains quickly; I need a solution.
Η μπαταρία του φορητού μου υπολογιστή αδειάζει γρήγορα· χρειάζομαι μια λύση.
(I mpa-ta-rí-a tou fo-ri-toú mou i-po-lo-gi-stí a-diá-zei grí-go-ra, hreiá-zo-mai mi-a lí-si.)

805. There's a software update available for my device.
Υπάρχει διαθέσιμη ενημέρωση λογισμικού για τη συσκευή μου.
(I-pár-hi di-a-thé-si-mi e-ni-mé-ro-si lo-gi-smi-koú gia ti sys-ke-ví mou.)

806. My email account got locked; I need to recover it.
Ο λογαριασμός μου στο ηλεκτρονικό ταχυδρομείο έχει κλειδωθεί· πρέπει να τον ανακτήσω.
(O lo-ga-ri-as-mós mou sto i-lek-tro-ni-kó ta-hi-dro-mí-o é-hei klei-do-thí; pré-pei na ton a-nak-tí-so.)

807. The screen on my tablet is cracked; I'm upset.
Η οθόνη του tablet μου έχει σπάσει· είμαι απογοητευμένος/η.
(I o-thó-ni tou tablet mou é-hei spá-si; eí-mai a-po-go-i-tev-me-nós/i.)

808. My webcam isn't working during video calls.
Η web κάμερά μου δεν λειτουργεί κατά τη διάρκεια των βιντεοκλήσεων.
(I web ká-me-rá mou den lei-tour-gí ka-tá ti diár-kei-a ton vin-te-o-klí-seon.)

809. My phone's storage is almost full; I need to clear it.
Η μνήμη του κινητού μου είναι σχεδόν γεμάτη· πρέπει να την καθαρίσω.
(I mní-mi tou ki-ni-tóu mou eí-nai scheidón ge-má-ti; pré-pei na tin ka-tha-rí-so.)

810.   I accidentally deleted important files; I need help.
       Διέγραψα κατά λάθος σημαντικά αρχεία· χρειάζομαι βοήθεια.
       (Di-é-grap-sa ka-tá lá-thos si-man-ti-ká ar-hí-a; hreiá-zo-mai
       voí-thei-a.)

       Fun Fact: The famous Greek salad is known in Greece as
       'Horiatiki,' which means 'village salad.'

811.   My smart home devices are not responding.
       Οι συσκευές του έξυπνου σπιτιού μου δεν ανταποκρίνονται.
       (I sys-ke-vés tou é-xi-pnou spi-ti-oú mou den
       an-ta-po-krí-non-tai.)

812.   The GPS on my navigation app is inaccurate.
       Το GPS στην εφαρμογή πλοήγησής μου δεν είναι ακριβές.
       (To GPS stin ef-ar-mo-gí plo-í-gi-sís mou den eí-nai a-kri-vés.)

813.   My antivirus software detected a threat; I'm worried.
       Το αντιικό μου λογισμικό ανίχνευσε μια απειλή· ανησυχώ.
       (To an-di-i-kó mou lo-gi-smi-kó a-ní-hnef-se mi-a a-peilí;
       a-ni-si-hó.)

814.   The touchscreen on my device is unresponsive.
       Η οθόνη αφής της συσκευής μου δεν ανταποκρίνεται.
       (I o-thó-ni afís tis sys-ke-vís mou den an-ta-po-krí-ne-tai.)

815.   My gaming console is displaying error messages.
       Η κονσόλα παιχνιδιών μου εμφανίζει μηνύματα σφάλματος.
       (I kon-só-la peh-ni-di-ón mou em-fa-ní-zei mi-ní-ma-ta
       sfál-ma-tos.)

       Fun Fact: Rebetiko, a genre of Greek folk music, is often
       referred to as the Greek blues.

816.   I'm locked out of my social media account.
       Έχω κλειδωθεί έξω από τον λογαριασμό μου στα κοινωνικά μέσα.
       (É-ho klei-do-thí é-xo apó ton lo-ga-ri-as-mó mou sta ki-no-ni-ká mé-sa.)

817.   The sound on my computer is distorted.
       Ο ήχος στον υπολογιστή μου είναι παραμορφωμένος.
       (O í-hos ston i-po-lo-gi-stí mou eí-nai pa-ra-mor-fo-mé-nos.)

818.   My email attachments won't open; it's frustrating.
       Τα συνημμένα στο email μου δεν ανοίγουν· είναι απογοητευτικό.
       (Ta si-ni-mé-na sto email mou den a-ní-goun· eí-nai a-po-go-i-tef-ti-kó.)

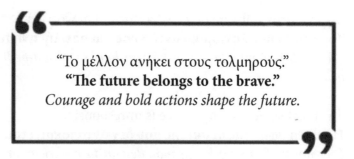

"Το μέλλον ανήκει στους τολμηρούς."
"The future belongs to the brave."
Courage and bold actions shape the future.

Cross Word Puzzle: Technology & Communication

(Provide the English translation for the following Greek words)

Down

1. - ΕΚΤΥΠΩΤΉΣ
3. - ΔΊΚΤΥΟ
4. - ΥΠΟΛΟΓΙΣΤΗΣ
6. - ΔΙΑΔΊΚΤΥΟ
7. - ΠΕΡΙΗΓΗΤΉΣ
8. - ΚΆΜΕΡΑ ΙΣΤΟΎ
10. - ΔΡΟΜΟΛΟΓΗΤΉΣ
12. - ΔΕΔΟΜΈΝΑ
13. - ΣΥΝΝΕΦΟ

Across

2. - ΟΘΌΝΗ
5. - ΚΡΥΠΤΟΛΟΓΊΑ
9. - ΦΟΡΤΙΣΤΉΣ
11. - ΠΛΗΚΤΡΟΛΌΓΙΟ
14. - ΕΦΑΡΜΟΓΈΣ
15. - ΕΊΣΟΔΟΣ
16. - ΜΠΑΤΑΡΊΑ

Correct Answers:

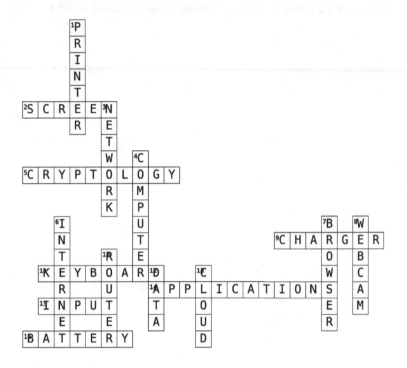

SPORTS & RECREATION

- DISCUSSING SPORTS, GAMES, & OUTDOOR ACTIVITIES -
- PARTICIPATING IN RECREATIONAL ACTIVITIES -
- EXPRESSING ENTHUSUASM OR FRUSTRATION -

Sports, Games, & Outdoor Activities

819.   I love playing soccer with my friends.
       Λατρεύω να παίζω ποδόσφαιρο με τους φίλους μου.
       (Lat-reúo na paízo po-dó-sfai-ro me tous fí-lous mou.)

820.   Basketball is a fast-paced and exciting sport.
       Το μπάσκετ είναι ένα γρήγορο και συναρπαστικό άθλημα.
       (To bá-sket eí-nai é-na grí-go-ro kai sy-nar-pa-sti-kó á-thli-ma.)

821.   Let's go for a hike in the mountains this weekend.
       Ας πάμε για πεζοπορία στα βουνά αυτό το σαββατοκύριακο.
       *(As pá-me gia pe-zo-po-rí-a sta vou-ná af-tó to
       sav-va-to-ký-ria-ko.)*

822.   Playing chess helps improve my strategic thinking.
       **Το παίξιμο σκάκι βοηθά στη βελτίωση της στρατηγικής
       σκέψης.**
       *(To paí-xi-mo ská-ki voi-thá sti vel-tí-o-si tis stra-ti-gi-kís
       ské-psis.)*

823.   I'm a fan of tennis; it requires a lot of skill.
       Είμαι φαν του τένις· απαιτεί πολλή δεξιότητα.
       (Eí-mai fan tou té-nis· a-pai-teí pol-lí dex-ió-ti-ta.)

824.   Are you up for a game of volleyball at the beach?
       Θέλετε να παίξουμε βόλεϊ στην παραλία;
       (Thé-le-te na paí-xou-me vó-lei stin pa-ra-lía?)

825.   Let's organize a game of ultimate frisbee.
       Ας οργανώσουμε ένα παιχνίδι απόλυτου φρίσμπι.
       (As or-ga-nó-sou-me é-na pai-hní-di a-pó-lu-tou frís-mbi.)

826. Baseball games are a great way to spend the afternoon.
Τα παιχνίδια μπέιζμπολ είναι ένας υπέροχος τρόπος να περάσεις το απόγευμα.
(*Ta pai-hní-dia béiz-mpol eí-nai é-nas y-pé-ro-chos tró-pos na pe-rá-sis to a-pó-gev-ma.*)

827. Camping in the wilderness is so peaceful.
Το κάμπινγκ στην άγρια φύση είναι τόσο ειρηνικό.
(*To kám-pingk stin á-gria fý-si eí-nai tó-so ei-ri-ni-kó.*)

828. I enjoy swimming in the local pool.
Απολαμβάνω το κολύμπι στην τοπική πισίνα.
(*A-po-lam-vá-no to ko-lým-pi stin to-pi-kí pi-sí-na.*)

829. I'm learning to play the guitar in my free time.
Μαθαίνω να παίζω κιθάρα στον ελεύθερο χρόνο μου.
(*Ma-thé-no na paí-zo ki-thá-ra ston e-leú-the-ro chró-no mou.*)

830. Skiing in the winter is an exhilarating experience.
Το σκι το χειμώνα είναι μια συναρπαστική εμπειρία.
(*To ski to hei-mó-na eí-nai mi-a sy-nar-pa-sti-kí em-peirí-a.*)

831. Going fishing by the lake is so relaxing.
Το ψάρεμα δίπλα στη λίμνη είναι τόσο χαλαρωτικό.
(*To psá-re-ma dí-pla sti lím-ni eí-nai tó-so cha-la-ro-ti-kó.*)

832. We should have a board game night with friends.
Πρέπει να οργανώσουμε μια βραδιά επιτραπέζιων παιχνιδιών με φίλους.
(*Pré-pei na or-ga-nó-sou-me mi-a vra-diá e-pi-tra-pé-zi-on pai-hni-di-ón me fí-lous.*)

> **Travel Story:** At the Acropolis, a tour guide said, "Η ιστορία ζει εδώ," meaning "History lives here," highlighting the monument's significance.

833.   Martial arts training keeps me fit and disciplined.
Η προπόνηση στις πολεμικές τέχνες με κρατά σε φόρμα και πειθαρχημένο.
(I pro-pó-ni-si stis po-le-mi-kés téch-nes me kra-tá se fór-ma kai pi-thar-chi-mé-no.)

834.   I'm a member of a local running club.
Είμαι μέλος ενός τοπικού δρομικού συλλόγου.
(Eí-mai mé-los e-nós to-pi-kóu dro-mi-kóu sy-ló-gou.)

835.   Playing golf is a great way to unwind.
Το παίξιμο γκολφ είναι ένας υπέροχος τρόπος για χαλάρωση.
(To paí-xi-mo golf eí-nai é-nas y-pé-ro-chos tró-pos gia cha-lá-ro-si.)

> **Idiomatic Expression:** "Έκοψε το νήμα." -
> Meaning: "Cut the thread (ended something)."
> (Literal translation: "Cut the thread.")

836.   Yoga classes help me stay flexible and calm.
Τα μαθήματα γιόγκα με βοηθούν να παραμείνω ευέλικτος και ήρεμος.
(Ta ma-thí-ma-ta yí-og-ka me voi-thoún na pa-ra-meí-no e-vé-lik-tos kai í-re-mos.)

837.   I can't wait to go snowboarding this season.
Ανυπομονώ να πάω για σνόουμπορντ αυτή τη σεζόν.
(A-ny-po-mo-nó na pá-o gia snó-ou-bornt af-tí ti se-zón.)

838.   Going kayaking down the river is an adventure.
Το καγιάκ στο ποτάμι είναι μια περιπέτεια.
(To ka-giák sto po-tá-mi eí-nai mi-a pe-ri-pé-tei-a.)

839.   Let's organize a picnic in the park.
Ας οργανώσουμε ένα πικνίκ στο πάρκο.
(As or-ga-nó-sou-me é-na pik-ník sto pá-rko.)

Participating in Recreational Activities

40. I enjoy painting landscapes as a hobby.
Απολαμβάνω τη ζωγραφική τοπίων ως χόμπι.
(A-po-lam-vá-no ti zo-gra-fi-kí to-pí-on os chó-mbi.)

41. Gardening is a therapeutic way to spend my weekends.
Η κηπουρική είναι μια θεραπευτική δραστηριότητα για τα σαββατοκύριακά μου.
(I ki-pou-ri-kí eí-nai mi-a the-ra-pef-ti-kí dras-ti-ri-ó-ti-ta gia ta sav-va-to-ký-ri-a-ká mou.)

42. Playing the piano is my favorite pastime.
Το παίξιμο πιάνου είναι το αγαπημένο μου παρελθόν.
(To paí-xi-mo piá-nou eí-nai to a-ga-pi-mé-no mou pa-rel-thón.)

43. Reading books helps me escape into different worlds.
Το διάβασμα βιβλίων με βοηθά να δραπετεύω σε διαφορετικούς κόσμους.
(To diá-vas-ma vi-vlí-on me voi-thá na dra-pe-tef-o se di-a-fo-re-ti-kús kós-mous.)

44. I'm a regular at the local dance classes.
Συχνάζω στα τοπικά μαθήματα χορού.
(Sy-chá-zo sta to-pi-ká ma-thí-ma-ta cho-rú.)

45. Woodworking is a skill I've been honing.
Η ξυλοτεχνία είναι μια δεξιότητα που βελτιώνω.
(I xy-lo-tech-ní-a eí-nai mi-a de-xi-ó-ti-ta pou ve-lió-no.)

> **Idiomatic Expression:** "Κάνω τον γύρο του θανάτου." -
> Meaning: "Going through a very tough time."
> (Literal translation: "I do the round of death.")

846. I find solace in birdwatching at the nature reserve.
Βρίσκω παρηγοριά στην παρατήρηση πουλιών στο φυσικό καταφύγιο.
(*Vrísko par-ee-go-ría stin pa-ra-tí-risi pou-lión sto fi-si-kó ka-ta-fý-gio.*)

847. Meditation and mindfulness keep me centered.
Η διαλογισμός και η επίγνωση με διατηρούν ισορροπημένο.
(*I dia-lo-gis-mós kai i e-píg-no-si me dia-ti-róun i-so-ro-pi-mé-no.*)

848. I've taken up photography to capture moments.
Άρχισα φωτογραφία για να απαθανατίζω στιγμές.
(*Ár-chi-sa fo-to-gra-fía gia na a-pa-tha-na-tí-zo stig-més.*)

849. Going to the gym is part of my daily routine.
Η προσέλευση στο γυμναστήριο είναι μέρος της καθημερινή μου ρουτίνας.
(*I pro-sé-lef-si sto gym-na-stí-rio eí-nai mé-ros tis ka-thi-me-ri-n mou rou-tí-nas.*)

850. Cooking new recipes is a creative outlet for me.
Το μαγείρεμα νέων συνταγών είναι δημιουργική διέξοδος για μένα.
(*To ma-gí-re-ma né-on syn-ta-gón eí-nai di-mi-our-gi-kí di-éx-o-dos gia mé-na.*)

851. Building model airplanes is a fascinating hobby.
Η κατασκευή μοντέλων αεροπλάνων είναι ένα γοητευτικό χόμπι.
(*I ka-ta-skef-í mon-té-lon ae-ro-plá-non eí-nai é-na go-i-tef-ti-kó chó-mbi.*)

852. I love attending art exhibitions and galleries.
Αγαπώ να πηγαίνω σε εκθέσεις τέχνης και γκαλερί.
(*A-ga-pó na pi-gaí-no se ek-thé-seis téch-nis kai ga-le-rí.*)

53. Collecting rare stamps has been a lifelong passion.
Η συλλογή σπάνιων γραμματοσήμων είναι πάθος μιας ζωής.
(I sy-logí spá-nion gram-ma-to-sí-mon eí-nai pá-thos mi-as zo-ís.)

54. I'm part of a community theater group.
Είμαι μέλος μιας θεατρικής ομάδας της κοινότητας.
(Eí-mai mé-los mi-as the-a-tri-kís o-má-das tis ki-nó-ti-tas.)

55. Birdwatching helps me connect with nature.
Η παρατήρηση πουλιών με βοηθά να συνδεθώ με τη φύση.
(I pa-ra-tí-ri-si pou-lión me voi-thá na syn-de-thó me ti fý-si.)

56. I'm an avid cyclist and explore new trails.
Είμαι ένθερμος ποδηλάτης και εξερευνώ νέα μονοπάτια.
(Eí-mai én-the-ros po-di-lá-tis kai ex-eref-nó né-a mo-no-pá-tia.)

57. Pottery classes allow me to express myself.
Τα μαθήματα κεραμικής μου επιτρέπουν να εκφράσω τον εαυτό μου.
(Ta ma-thí-ma-ta ke-ra-mi-kís mou e-pi-tré-poun na ek-frá-so ton ea-f-tó mou.)

58. Playing board games with family is a tradition.
Το παίξιμο παιχνιδιών σανίδας με την οικογένεια είναι παράδοση.
(To pá-ixi-mo pai-chni-di-ón sa-ní-das me tin oi-ko-gé-ni-a eí-nai pa-rá-do-si.)

59. I'm practicing mindfulness through meditation.
Εξασκώ την επίγνωση μέσω του διαλογισμού.
(Ex-as-kó tin e-píg-no-si mé-so tou dia-lo-gis-moú.)

860. I enjoy long walks in the park with my dog.
Απολαμβάνω μακριές βόλτες στο πάρκο με τον σκύλο μου.
(*Apo-lam-vá-no mak-riés vól-tes sto pá-rko me ton ský-lo mou.*)

> **Travel Story:** In a fish market in Piraeus, a fishmonger said, "Η θάλασσα είναι γενναιόδωρη," translating to "The sea is generous," appreciating the ocean's bounty.

Expressing Enthusiasm or Frustration

861. I'm thrilled we won the championship!
Είμαι ενθουσιασμένος που κερδίσαμε το πρωτάθλημα!
(*Eí-mai enthousi-as-mé-nos pou ker-dí-sa-me to pro-tá-thli-ma!*)

862. Scoring that goal felt amazing.
Το σκοράρισμα αυτού του γκολ ήταν απίστευτο.
(*To sko-rá-ris-ma af-tou tou gol í-tan a-pís-teu-to.*)

863. It's so frustrating when we lose a game.
Είναι τόσο απογοητευτικό όταν χάνουμε ένα παιχνίδι.
(*Eí-nai tó-so a-po-goi-tef-ti-kó ó-tan chá-nou-me é-na pai-chní-di.*)

864. I can't wait to play again next week.
Δεν μπορώ να περιμένω να παίξω ξανά την επόμενη εβδομάδα.
(*Den bo-ró na pe-ri-mé-no na pái-xo xaná tin e-pó-me-ni ev-do-má-da.*)

> **Fun Fact:** The concept of the atom was first conceived by the ancient Greek philosopher Democritus.

365. Our team's performance was outstanding.
      Η απόδοση της ομάδας μας ήταν εξαιρετική.
      (*I a-pó-do-si tis o-má-das mas í-tan ex-ai-re-ti-kí.*)

366. We need to practice more; we keep losing.
      Χρειάζεται να προπονούμαστε περισσότερο· συνεχίζουμε να χάνουμε.
      (*Chreiá-ze-tai na pro-po-noú-mas-te pe-ris-só-te-ro; sy-ne-chí-zou-me na chá-nou-me.*)

367. I'm over the moon about our victory!
      Είμαι πολύ χαρούμενος για την νίκη μας!
      (*Eí-mai po-lý cha-roú-me-nos gia tin ní-ki mas!*)

      Language Learning Tip: Follow Greek News - Try to read or watch the news in Greek to get accustomed to formal language.

368. I'm an avid cyclist and explore new trails.
      Είμαι παθιασμένος ποδηλάτης και εξερευνώ νέα μονοπάτια.
      (*Eí-mai pa-thi-as-mé-nos po-di-lá-tis kai ex-e-rev-nó né-a mo-no-pá-tia.*)

369. The referee's decision was unfair.
      Η απόφαση του διαιτητή ήταν άδικη.
      (*I a-pó-fa-si tou di-ai-ti-tí í-tan á-di-ki.*)

870. We've been on a winning streak lately.
      Έχουμε πετύχει μια σειρά νικών τελευταία.
      (*É-chou-me pe-tý-chei mi-a se-i-rá ni-kón te-lef-taí-a.*)

871. I'm disappointed in our team's performance.
      Είμαι απογοητευμένος από την απόδοση της ομάδας μας.
      (*Eí-mai a-po-goi-tef-me-nós apó tin a-pó-do-si tis o-má-das mas.*)

872.   The adrenaline rush during the race was incredible.
         Η αδρεναλίνη κατά τη διάρκεια του αγώνα ήταν απίστευτη.
         (*I ad-re-na-lí-ni ka-tá ti diár-kei-a tou a-gó-na í-tan a-pís-tef-ti.*)

873.   We need to step up our game to compete.
         Πρέπει να ανεβάσουμε το παιχνίδι μας για να
         ανταγωνιστούμε.
         (*Pré-pei na a-ne-vá-sou-me to pai-chní-di mas gia na*
         an-ta-go-ni-stoú-me.)

874.   Winning the tournament was a dream come true.
         Η κατάκτηση του τουρνουά ήταν η πραγματοποίηση ενός
         ονείρου.
         (*I ka-ták-ti-si tou tour-nou-á í-tan i prag-ma-to-poí-i-si e-nós*
         o-neí-rou.)

875.   I was so close to scoring a goal.
         Ήμουν τόσο κοντά στο να σημειώσω γκολ.
         (*Í-moun tó-so kon-tá sto na si-mei-ó-so gol.*)

876.   We should celebrate our recent win.
         Θα πρέπει να γιορτάσουμε την πρόσφατη νίκη μας.
         (*Tha pré-pei na gio-rtá-sou-me tin pró-sfa-ti ní-ki mas.*)

877.   Losing by a narrow margin is frustrating.
         Η ήττα με μικρή διαφορά είναι απογοητευτική.
         (*I ít-ta me mi-krí dia-fo-rá eí-nai a-po-goi-tef-ti-kí.*)

878.   Let's train harder to improve our skills.
         Ας προπονηθούμε πιο σκληρά για να βελτιώσουμε τις
         δεξιότητές μας.
         (*As pro-po-ni-thoú-me pio skli-rá gia na vel-tió-sou-me tis*
         dexi-ó-ti-tés mas.)

79. The match was intense from start to finish.
Ο αγώνας ήταν έντονος από την αρχή έως το τέλος.
(O a-gó-nas í-tan én-tonos a-pó tin ar-chí éos to té-los.)

80. I'm proud of our team's sportsmanship.
Είμαι περήφανος για το αθλητικό πνεύμα της ομάδας μας.
(Eí-mai pe-rí-fa-nos gia to ath-li-ti-kó pneú-ma tis o-má-das mas.)

81. We've faced tough competition this season.
Αντιμετωπίσαμε δύσκολο ανταγωνισμό αυτή τη σεζόν.
(An-ti-me-to-pí-sa-me dý-sko-lo an-ta-go-nis-mó af-tí ti se-zón.)

82. I'm determined to give it my all in the next game.
Είμαι αποφασισμένος να δώσω τα πάντα στο επόμενο παιχνίδι.
(Eí-mai a-po-fa-sis-mé-nos na dó-so ta pán-ta sto e-pó-me-no pai-chní-di.)

"Η ζωή είναι ένα ταξίδι."
"Life is a journey."
Life is a continuous process of growth and experiences.

Mini Lesson:
Basic Grammar Principles in Greek #3

Introduction:

Welcome to the third installment of our journey through Greek grammar. Building on the basics and the intermediate concepts we've discussed, this lesson will dive into some of the more intricate elements of Greek grammar. These will help you gain a deeper understanding and improve both your conversational and written Greek.

1. The Optative Mood:

Greek has a mood called the "optative," which is used to express wishes or potentiality. It's more common in ancient Greek but is still seen in modern literary or formal contexts.

- *Ευχόμουν να είχα περισσότερο χρόνο. (I wish I had more time.)*

2. Causative Constructions:

To express causing someone to do something, Greek uses a combination of verbs like "κάνω" (to make/do) with another verb in the infinitive.

- *Τον έκανα να γελάσει. (I made him laugh.)*

. Reduplication:

.eduplication involves repeating a syllable to form a new word or a ifferent verb aspect. This is more frequent in older forms of Greek but till appears in some modern terms.

- *Γελώ-γελάω (to laugh - to keep laughing)*

. Use of "έχω" for Perfect Tenses:

imilar to English "have" in perfect tenses, "έχω" is used in Greek to orm various perfect constructions.

- *Έχω διαβάσει το βιβλίο. (I have read the book.)*

. Direct and Indirect Speech:

Greek distinguishes between direct and indirect speech, often using ότι" for indirect.

- *Είπε ότι θα έρθει. (He said that he would come.)*

. Conditional Clauses:

Conditional clauses in Greek are formed with "εάν" (if) and various enses depending on the condition's likelihood.

- *Εάν βρέξει, θα μείνουμε σπίτι. (If it rains, we will stay home.)*

7. Emphasis through Word Order:

Greek uses flexible word order to place emphasis. The element placed at the beginning of the sentence usually carries the most weight.

- *Τα δώρα, τα έφερε ο Νίκος. (The gifts were brought by Nick.)*

Conclusion:

These advanced aspects of Greek grammar open up new avenues for expressing complex ideas and nuances. Understanding them requires practice and patience, but mastering these will significantly enhance your fluency and comprehension. Keep practicing and immersing yourself in the language - Καλή τύχη! (Good luck!)

TRANSPORT & DIRECTIONS

- ASKING FOR AND GIVING DIRECTIONS -
- USING TRANSPORTATION-RELATED PHRASES   -

Asking for and Giving Directions

883.   Can you tell me how to get to the nearest subway station?
        **Μπορείτε να μου πείτε πώς να φτάσω στον πλησιέστερο
        σταθμό μετρό;**
        *(Bo-reí-te na mou peí-te pós na ftá-so ston pli-sié-ste-ro
        stath-mó me-tró?)*

884.   Excuse me, where's the bus stop for Route 25?
        Συγγνώμη, πού είναι η στάση λεωφορείου για τη διαδρομή 25
        *(Syng-nó-mi, poú eí-nai i stá-si le-o-fo-reí-ou gia ti
        di-a-dro-mí 25?)*

885.   Could you give me directions to the city center?
        Μπορείτε να μου δώσετε οδηγίες για το κέντρο της πόλης;
        (Bo-reí-te na mou dó-se-te o-di-gí-es gia to kén-tro tis pó-lis?)

886.   I'm looking for a good place to eat around here. Any
        recommendations?
        **Ψάχνω για ένα καλό μέρος για φαγητό εδώ γύρω. Έχετε καμία
        σύσταση;**
        *(Psách-no gia é-na ka-ló mé-ros gia fa-gi-tó e-dó gý-ro. É-che-te
        ka-mí-a sý-sta-si?)*

887.   Which way is the nearest pharmacy?
        Ποιος είναι ο πλησιέστερος δρόμος για το φαρμακείο;
        (Poi-os eí-nai o pli-siés-te-ros dró-mos gia to far-ma-keí-o?)

888.   How do I get to the airport from here?
        Πώς θα πάω στο αεροδρόμιο από εδώ;
        (Pós tha pá-o sto ae-ro-dró-mio apó e-dó?)

89. Can you point me to the nearest ATM?
Μπορείτε να με κατευθύνετε προς το πλησιέστερο ATM;
(*Bo-reí-te na me ka-tef-thý-ne-te pros to pli-siés-te-ro ATM?*)

90. I'm lost. Can you help me find my way back to the hotel?
Έχω χαθεί. Μπορείτε να με βοηθήσετε να βρω το δρόμο πίσω για το ξενοδοχείο;
(*É-cho cha-thí. Bo-reí-te na me voi-thí-se-te na vro to dró-mo pí-so gia to xe-no-do-cheí-o?*)

91. Where's the closest gas station?
Πού είναι το πλησιέστερο βενζινάδικο;
(*Poú eí-nai to pli-siés-te-ro ven-zi-ná-di-ko?*)

92. Is there a map of the city available?
Υπάρχει διαθέσιμος χάρτης της πόλης;
(*Y-pár-chei di-a-thé-si-mos chár-tis tis pó-lis?*)

93. How far is it to the train station from here?
Πόσο μακριά είναι ο σιδηροδρομικός σταθμός από εδώ;
(*Pó-so mak-riá eí-nai o si-di-ro-dro-mi-kós stath-mós apó e-dó?*)

94. Which exit should I take to reach the shopping mall?
Ποια έξοδο πρέπει να πάρω για να φτάσω στο εμπορικό κέντρο;
(*Poia é-xo-do pré-pei na pá-ro gia na ftá-so sto em-po-ri-kó kén-tro?*)

95. Where can I find a taxi stand around here?
Πού μπορώ να βρω στάση ταξί εδώ γύρω;
(*Poú bo-ró na vro stá-si ta-xí e-dó gý-ro?*)

896. Can you direct me to the main tourist attractions?
Μπορείτε να μου δείξετε το δρόμο για τα κύρια τουριστικά αξιοθέατα;
(*Bo-reí-te na mou deí-xe-te to dró-mo gia ta ký-ria tou-ri-sti-ká a-xio-thé-a-ta?*)

> **Fun Fact:** The Apokries, a Greek carnival period, leads up to Lent and is marked by feasting and dancing.

897. I need to go to the hospital. Can you provide directions?
Χρειάζομαι να πάω στο νοσοκομείο. Μπορείτε να μου δώσετ οδηγίες;
(*Chre-iá-zo-mai na pá-o sto no-so-ko-meí-o. Bo-reí-te na mou dó-se-te o-di-gí-es?*)

898. Is there a park nearby where I can go for a walk?
Υπάρχει κοντινό πάρκο για να περπατήσω;
(*Y-pár-chei kon-ti-nó pá-rko gia na per-pa-tí-so?*)

899. Which street should I take to reach the museum?
Ποιο δρόμο πρέπει να πάρω για να φτάσω στο μουσείο;
(*Pio dró-mo pré-pei na pá-ro gia na ftá-so sto mou-seí-o?*)

900. How do I get to the concert venue?
Πώς θα πάω στον χώρο της συναυλίας;
(*Pós tha pá-o ston chó-ro tis sy-na-vli-ás?*)

901. Can you guide me to the nearest public restroom?
Μπορείτε να με κατευθύνετε στις πλησιέστερες δημόσιες τουαλέτες;
(*Bo-reí-te na me ka-tef-thý-ne-te stis pli-siés-te-res di-mó-sies tou-a-lé-tes?*)

02.   Where's the best place to catch a cab in this area?
       Πού είναι το καλύτερο σημείο για να βρω ταξί σε αυτή την
       περιοχή;
       (Poú eí-nai to ka-lý-te-ro si-mí-o gia na vro ta-xí se af-tí tin
       pe-ri-o-chí?)

Buying Tickets

03.   I'd like to buy a one-way ticket to downtown, please.
       Θα ήθελα να αγοράσω εισιτήριο μονής διαδρομής για το
       κέντρο, παρακαλώ.
       (Tha í-the-la na a-go-rá-so ei-si-tí-rio mo-nís di-a-dro-mís gia to
       kén-tro, pa-ra-ka-ló?)

04.   How much is a round-trip ticket to the airport?
       Πόσο κοστίζει ένα εισιτήριο με επιστροφή για το αεροδρόμιο;
       (Pó-so kos-tí-zei é-na ei-si-tí-rio me e-pis-tro-fí gia to
       ae-ro-dró-mio?)

05.   Do you accept credit cards for ticket purchases?
       Δέχεστε πιστωτικές κάρτες για την αγορά εισιτηρίων;
       (Dé-che-ste pis-to-ti-kés kár-tes gia tin a-go-rá ei-si-ti-ri-ón?)

06.   Can I get a student discount on this train ticket?
       Μπορώ να έχω φοιτητική έκπτωση για αυτό το εισιτήριο
       τρένου;
       (Bo-ró na é-cho foi-ti-ti-kí ék-p-to-si gia af-tó to ei-si-tí-rio
       tré-nou?)

07.   Is there a family pass available for the bus?
       Υπάρχει διαθέσιμο οικογενειακό πέρασμα για το λεωφορείο;
       (Y-pár-chei di-a-thé-si-mo oi-ko-ge-nei-a-kó pé-ras-ma gia to
       le-o-fo-reí-o?)

908. What's the fare for a child on the subway?
Πόσο κοστίζει το εισιτήριο για παιδί στο μετρό;
(Pó-so kos-tí-zei to ei-si-tí-rio gia pe-di stó me-tró?)

909. Are there any senior citizen discounts for tram tickets?
Υπάρχουν έκπτωσεις για τους ηλικιωμένους στα εισιτήρια το
τραμ;
(Y-pár-choun ék-p-to-seis gia tous i-li-ki-o-mé-nous sta ei-si-tí-rie
tou tram?)

910. Do I need to make a reservation for the express train?
Χρειάζεται να κάνω κράτηση για τον εκπρέσσο;
(Chre-iá-ze-tai na ká-no krá-ti-si gia ton ek-prés-so?)

911. Can I upgrade to first class on this flight?
Μπορώ να αναβαθμίσω σε πρώτη θέση σε αυτή την πτήση;
(Bo-ró na a-na-va-thmí-so se pró-ti thé-si se af-tí tin ptí-si?)

912. Are there any extra fees for luggage on this bus?
Υπάρχουν επιπλέον τέλη για αποσκευές σε αυτό το
λεωφορείο;
(Y-pár-choun e-pi-plé-on té-li gia a-po-ske-vés se af-tó to
le-o-fo-reí-o?)

913. I'd like to book a sleeper car for the overnight train.
Θέλω να κλείσω ένα υπνοβάγονο για το νυχτερινό τρένο.
(Thé-lo na klí-so é-na yp-no-vá-go-no gia to ny-chte-ri-nó tré-no?

914. What's the schedule for the next ferry to the island?
Ποιο είναι το πρόγραμμα για το επόμενο φέρι προς το νησί;
(Pi-o eí-nai to pró-gram-ma gia to e-pó-me-no fé-ri pros to ni-sí?)

915. Are there any available seats on the evening bus to the beach?
Υπάρχουν διαθέσιμες θέσεις στο βραδινό λεωφορείο για την παραλία;
(*Y-pár-choun di-a-thé-si-mes thé-seis sto vra-di-nó le-o-fo-reí-o gia tin pa-ra-lía?*)

916. Can I pay for my metro ticket with a mobile app?
Μπορώ να πληρώσω το εισιτήριο του μετρό με μια κινητή εφαρμογή;
(*Bo-ró na pli-ró-so to ei-si-tí-rio tou me-tró me mi-a ki-ni-tí e-far-mo-gí?*)

917. Is there a discount for purchasing tickets online?
Υπάρχει έκπτωση για την αγορά εισιτηρίων μέσω διαδικτύου;
(*Y-pár-chei ék-p-to-si gia tin a-go-rá ei-si-ti-rí-on mé-so di-adik-tý-ou?*)

918. How much is the parking fee at the train station?
Πόσο κοστίζει το τέλος στάθμευσης στον σταθμό τρένων;
(*Pó-so kos-tí-zei to té-los státh-meu-sis ston sta-thmó tré-non?*)

919. I'd like to reserve two seats for the next shuttle bus.
Θέλω να κρατήσω δύο θέσεις για το επόμενο λεωφορείο μεταφοράς.
(*Thé-lo na kra-tí-so dýo thé-seis gia to e-pó-me-no le-o-fo-reí-o me-ta-fo-rás?*)

920. Do I need to validate my ticket before boarding the tram?
Χρειάζεται να επικυρώσω το εισιτήριό μου πριν μπω στο τραμ;
(*Chre-iá-ze-tai na e-pi-ky-ró-so to ei-si-tí-rió mou prin mpo sto tram?*)

921. Can I buy a monthly pass for the subway?
Μπορώ να αγοράσω μηνιαίο εισιτήριο για το μετρό;
(*Bo-ró na a-go-rá-so mi-ni-aí-o ei-si-tí-rio gia to me-tró?*)

922. Are there any group rates for the boat tour?
Υπάρχουν ομαδικές τιμές για την περιήγηση με το καράβι;
(*Y-pár-choun o-ma-di-kés ti-més gia tin pe-ri-í-ge-si me to ka-rá-vi?*)

> **Travel Story:** At a grape harvest in Nemea, a vintner said, "Η ζωή είναι σαν κρασί," meaning "Life is like wine, comparing life's richness to wine's complexity.

Arranging Travel

923. I need to book a flight to Paris for next week.
Χρειάζομαι να κλείσω μια πτήση για το Παρίσι για την επόμενη εβδομάδα.
(*Chre-iá-zo-mai na klí-so mia ptí-si gia to Pa-rí-si gia tin e-pó-me-ni ev-do-má-da.*)

924. What's the earliest departure time for the high-speed train?
Ποια είναι η νωρίτερη ώρα αναχώρησης για το ταχύτατο τρένο;
(*Pi-a eí-nai i no-rí-te-ri ó-ra a-na-chó-ri-sis gia to ta-chý-ta-to tré-no?*)

925. Can I change my bus ticket to a later time?
Μπορώ να αλλάξω το εισιτήριο του λεωφορείου για αργότερη ώρα;
(*Bo-ró na al-lá-xo to ei-si-tí-rio tou le-o-fo-reí-ou gia ar-gó-te-ri ó-ra?*)

926. I'd like to rent a car for a week.
Θα ήθελα να ενοικιάσω ένα αυτοκίνητο για μια εβδομάδα.
(*Tha í-the-la na e-noi-kiá-so é-na af-to-kí-ni-to gia mia ev-do-má-da.*)

27. Is there a direct flight to New York from here?
Υπάρχει απευθείας πτήση για τη Νέα Υόρκη από εδώ;
(Y-pár-chei a-pef-theí-as ptí-si gia ti Né-a Yór-ki apó e-dó?)

28. I need to cancel my reservation for the cruise.
Χρειάζομαι να ακυρώσω την κράτησή μου για την κρουαζιέρα.
(Chre-iá-zo-mai na a-ky-ró-so tin krá-ti-sí mou gia tin krou-a-zié-ra.)

29. Can you help me find a reliable taxi service for airport transfers?
Μπορείτε να με βοηθήσετε να βρω μια αξιόπιστη ταξί υπηρεσία για μεταφορές αεροδρομίου;
(Bo-reí-te na me vo-i-thí-se-te na vro mia a-xió-pi-sti ta-xí y-pe-re-sí-a gia me-ta-fo-rés ae-ro-dro-mí-ou?)

30. I'm interested in a guided tour of the city.
How can I arrange that?
Ενδιαφέρομαι για μια ξενάγηση στην πόλη. Πώς μπορώ να το οργανώσω;
(En-di-a-fé-ro-mai gia mia kse-ná-gi-si stin pó-li. Pós bo-ró na to or-ga-nó-so?)

31. Do you have any information on overnight buses to the capital?
Έχετε κάποιες πληροφορίες για νυχτερινά λεωφορεία προς την πρωτεύουσα;
(É-che-te ká-pi-es pli-ro-fo-rí-es gia ny-chte-ri-ná le-o-fo-reí-a pros tin pro-te-ú-ou-sa?)

32. I'd like to purchase a travel insurance policy for my trip.
Θα ήθελα να αγοράσω μια ασφαλιστική πολιτική ταξιδιού για το ταξίδι μου.
(Tha í-the-la na a-go-rá-so mia as-fa-li-sti-kí po-li-ti-kí ta-xi-di-ou gia to ta-xí-di mou.)

933. Can you recommend a good travel agency for vacation packages?
Μπορείτε να προτείνετε μια καλή τουριστική γραφείο για πακέτα διακοπών;
(Bo-reí-te na pro-teí-ne-te mi-a ka-lí tou-ri-sti-kí gra-feí-o gia pa-ké-ta di-a-ko-pón?)

934. I need a seat on the evening ferry to the island.
Χρειάζομαι μια θέση στο βραδινό πλοίο για το νησί.
(Chreiá-zo-mai mi-a thé-si sto vra-di-nó ploí-o gia to ni-sí.)

935. How can I check the departure times for international flights?
Πώς μπορώ να ελέγξω τις ώρες αναχώρησης για διεθνείς πτήσεις;
(Pós bo-ró na e-lé-xo tis ó-res a-na-chó-ri-sis gia di-eth-neís ptí-seis?)

936. Is there a shuttle service from the hotel to the train station?
Υπάρχει υπηρεσία λεωφορείου από το ξενοδοχείο προς τον σταθμό τρένων;
(Ypár-chei y-pi-re-sí-a le-o-fo-reí-ou apó to xe-no-do-cheí-o pros ton sta-thmó tré-non?)

937. I'd like to charter a private boat for a day trip.
Θα ήθελα να ναυλώσω ένα ιδιωτικό σκάφος για μια ημερήσια εκδρομή.
(Tha í-the-la na nau-ló-so é-na i-dio-ti-kó ská-fos gia mi-a i-me-rí-sia ek-dro-mí.)

938. Can you assist me in booking a vacation rental apartment?
Μπορείτε να με βοηθήσετε στην κράτηση ενός διαμερίσματος για διακοπές;
(Bo-reí-te na me voi-thí-se-te stin krá-ti-si e-nós di-a-me-rís-ma-tos gia di-a-ko-pés?)

39. I need to arrange transportation for a group of 20 people.
Χρειάζομαι να οργανώσω μεταφορά για μια ομάδα από είκοσι άτομα.
(*Chreiá-zo-mai na or-ga-nó-so me-ta-fo-rá gia mi-a o-má-da apó eí-ko-si á-to-ma.*)

40. What's the best way to get from the airport to the city center?
Ποιός είναι ο καλύτερος τρόπος για να πάω από το αεροδρόμιο στο κέντρο της πόλης;
(*Poi-ós eí-nai o ka-lý-te-ros tró-pos gia na pá-o apó to ae-ro-dró-mio sto kén-tro tis pó-lis?*)

41. Can you help me find a pet-friendly accommodation option?
Μπορείτε να με βοηθήσετε να βρω κατάλυμα που δέχεται κατοικίδια;
(*Bo-reí-te na me voi-thí-se-te na vro ka-tá-ly-ma pou dé-che-tai ka-toi-kí-di-a?*)

42. I'd like to plan a road trip itinerary for a scenic drive.
Θα ήθελα να σχεδιάσω ένα δρομολόγιο για μια γραφική διαδρομή.
(*Tha í-the-la na sche-diá-so é-na dro-mo-ló-gio gia mi-a gra-fi-kí di-a-dro-mí.*)

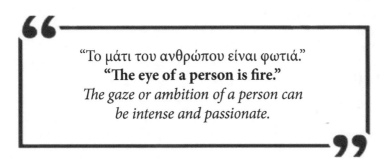

"Το μάτι του ανθρώπου είναι φωτιά."
"The eye of a person is fire."
*The gaze or ambition of a person can
be intense and passionate.*

Word Search Puzzle: Transport & Directions

CAR
ΑΥΤΟΚΙΝΗΤΟ
BUS
ΛΕΩΦΟΡΕΙΟ
AIRPORT
ΑΕΡΟΔΡΟΜΙΟ
SUBWAY
ΜΕΤΡΟ
TAXI
ΤΑΞΙ
STREET
ΟΔΟΣ
MAP
ΧΑΡΤΗΣ
DIRECTION
ΚΑΤΕΥΘΥΝΣΗ
TRAFFIC
ΚΙΝΗΤΙΚΟΤΗΤΑ
PARKING
ΠΑΡΚΙΝΓΚ
PEDESTRIAN
ΠΕΖΟΣ
HIGHWAY
ΑΥΤΟΚΙΝΗΤΟΔΡΟΜΟΣ
BRIDGE
ΓΕΦΥΡΑ
TICKET
ΕΙΣΙΤΗΡΙΟ

```
D P C P Σ S R S I T K V F N K
S T T O S H W J O D A R S O I
W V Δ M P Y T S O T U Ξ N I N
H O W T W Q E P D W E P I T H
Σ T R A F F I C A T X B Y C T
A O C R R C H B A X H P Y E I
V Y I F D Z A I J S O P D R K
V D T M I N Q Y R L O Λ S I O
T Γ N O O Y B F S I E S S D T
F S E X K P O X C Ω E U Y Y H
N U W Φ T I Δ W Φ U U L L I T
T B D P Y N N O B R I D G E A
C Y B V I P P H P M S P G H C
O I U W O E A F T E A B Σ H Y
A C S P I S V U M O A N Q A T
E P T O U Z M C T Q Y P W Z I
W E Y S W L O B C Θ A H Y E C
M A Q P Z N V G Y R G W I W K
T R O P R I A E K I Z Σ R J E
N C A R T I T I H B I G D X T
D R P L A A N A R T M L Y X S
S L T W K G Z M H T X L W I R
V C U R S F X P O Σ S B U Z Q
F J E Z T S I H J O O E B E Q
D I S U R O Y X L Z Y D D X P
T A X I E C O W R E A D J E N
I L S A E P A M Q Π W Z M O P
O J C W T U C C N S B R R Q T
K Γ N I K P A Π G Z U N M R Y
D T A X J J D S B L S S R P F
```

Correct Answers:

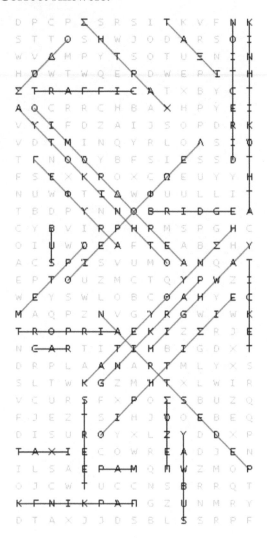

SPECIAL OCCASIONS

- EXPRESSING WELL WISHES AND CONGRATULATIONS -
- CELEBRATIONS AND CULTURAL EVENTS -
- GIVING AND RECEIVING GIFTS -

Expressing Well Wishes & Congratulations

943.   Congratulations on your graduation!
       Συγχαρητήρια για την αποφοίτησή σου!
       (Syn-cha-ri-tí-ria gia tin a-po-foí-ti-sí sou!)

944.   Best wishes for a long and happy marriage.
       Τις καλύτερες ευχές για έναν μακρύ και ευτυχισμένο γάμο.
       (Tis ka-lý-te-res ef-chés gia é-nan ma-krý kai ef-ty-chis-mé-no gá-mo.)

945.   Happy anniversary to a wonderful couple.
       Ευτυχισμένη επέτειο σε ένα υπέροχο ζευγάρι.
       (Ef-ty-chis-mé-ni e-pé-ti-o se é-na y-pé-ro-cho ze-vgá-ri.)

946.   Wishing you a speedy recovery.
       Σου εύχομαι γρήγορη ανάρρωση.
       (Sou éf-cho-mai grí-go-ri a-nár-ro-si.)

947.   Congratulations on your new job!
       Συγχαρητήρια για την καινούργια σου δουλειά!
       (Syn-cha-ri-tí-ria gia tin ke-noúr-gia sou dou-lei-á!)

> **Travel Story:** On a boat tour around Zakynthos, the guide pointed out, "Η φύση είναι ο καλύτερος ζωγράφος," meaning "Nature is the best painter," admiring the natural beauty.

948.   May your retirement be filled with joy and relaxation.
       Εύχομαι η συνταξιοδότησή σου να είναι γεμάτη χαρά και χαλάρωση.
       (Éf-cho-mai i syn-ta-xio-dó-ti-sí sou na eí-nai ge-má-ti cha-rá ka cha-lá-ro-si.)

49. Best wishes on your engagement.
    Τις καλύτερες ευχές για τον αρραβώνα σου.
    (*Tis ka-lý-te-res ef-chés gia ton ar-ra-vó-na sou.*)

50. Happy birthday! Have an amazing day.
    Χαρούμενα γενέθλια! Να έχεις μια καταπληκτική μέρα.
    (*Cha-roú-me-na ge-né-thli-a! Na é-cheis mi-a ka-ta-plek-ti-kí mé-ra.*)

> **Cultural Insight:** Ancient Greek myths, featuring gods, heroes, and magical creatures, play a significant role in cultural identity.

51. Wishing you success in your new venture.
    Σου εύχομαι επιτυχία στην καινούργια σου επιχείρηση.
    (*Sou éf-cho-mai e-pi-ty-chí-a stin ke-noúr-gia sou e-pi-chí-ri-si.*)

52. Congratulations on your promotion!
    Συγχαρητήρια για την προαγωγή σου!
    (*Syn-cha-ri-tí-ria gia tin pro-a-go-gí sou!*)

53. Good luck on your exam—you've got this!
    Καλή τύχη στις εξετάσεις σου - το έχεις αυτό!
    (*Ka-lí tý-chi stis e-xe-tá-seis sou - to é-cheis af-tó!*)

54. Best wishes for a safe journey.
    Τις καλύτερες ευχές για ένα ασφαλές ταξίδι.
    (*Tis ka-lý-te-res ef-chés gia é-na as-fa-lés ta-xí-di.*)

55. Happy retirement! Enjoy your newfound freedom.
    Ευτυχισμένη συνταξιοδότηση! Απόλαυσε τη νέα σου ελευθερία.
    (*Ef-ty-chis-mé-ni syn-ta-xio-dó-ti-si! A-pó-lau-se ti né-a sou e-lef-the-rí-a.*)

956. Congratulations on your new home.
Συγχαρητήρια για το νέο σπίτι σου.
(Syn-cha-ri-tí-ria gia to néo spí-ti sou.)

957. Wishing you a lifetime of love and happiness.
Εύχομαι μια ζωή γεμάτη αγάπη και ευτυχία.
(Éf-cho-mai mi-a zo-í ge-má-ti a-gá-pi kai ef-ty-chí-a.)

958. Best wishes on your upcoming wedding.
Τις καλύτερες ευχές για τον επικείμενο γάμο σας.
(Tis ka-lý-te-res ef-chés gia ton e-pi-kí-me-no gá-mo sas.)

959. Congratulations on the arrival of your baby.
Συγχαρητήρια για την άφιξη του μωρού σας.
(Syn-cha-ri-tí-ria gia tin á-fi-xi tou mo-roú sas.)

960. Sending you warmest thoughts and prayers.
Στέλνω τις θερμότερες σκέψεις και προσευχές μου.
(Stél-no tis ther-mó-te-res skép-seis kai pro-sef-chés mou.)

961. Happy holidays and a joyful New Year!
Καλές γιορτές και ένα χαρούμενο Νέο Έτος!
(Ka-lés yior-tés kai é-na cha-roú-me-no Néo É-tos!)

962. Wishing you a wonderful and prosperous future.
Εύχομαι ένα υπέροχο και ευημερούν μέλλον.
(Éf-cho-mai é-na y-pé-ro-cho kai e-vi-me-roún mél-lon.)

> **Idiomatic Expression:** "Κλείνω το μάτι." -
> Meaning: "Turn a blind eye or wink."
> (Literal translation: "I close the eye.")

Celebrations & Cultural Events

963. I'm excited to attend the festival this weekend.
Ανυπομονώ να πάω στο φεστιβάλ αυτό το σαββατοκύριακο.
(A-ni-po-mo-nó na pá-o sto fes-ti-vál af-tó to sav-va-to-ký-ri-a-ko.)

964. Let's celebrate this special occasion together.
Ας γιορτάσουμε μαζί αυτή την ξεχωριστή περίσταση.
(As yior-tá-sou-me ma-zí af-tí tin xe-cho-ris-tí pe-rís-ta-si.)

> **Fun Fact:** The Greek tortoise is a species native to the region and is one of the world's oldest tortoise species.

965. The cultural parade was a vibrant and colorful experience.
Η πολιτιστική παρέλαση ήταν μια ζωντανή και πολύχρωμη εμπειρία.
(I po-li-tis-ti-kí pa-ré-la-si í-tan mi-a zon-da-ní kai po-lí-chro-mi em-pi-ri-á.)

966. I look forward to the annual family reunion.
Ανυπομονώ για την ετήσια οικογενειακή συνάντηση.
(A-ni-po-mo-nó gia tin e-tí-sia i-ko-ge-nei-a-kí syn-án-ti-si.)

967. The fireworks display at the carnival was spectacular.
Η πυροτεχνηματική επίδειξη στο καρναβάλι ήταν θεαματική.
(I pi-ro-teh-ni-ma-ti-ki e-pí-dei-xi sto kar-na-vá-li í-tan the-a-ma-ti-kí.)

968. It's always a blast at the neighborhood block party.
Είναι πάντα ένας πύραυλος στο πάρτι της γειτονιάς.
(Í-ne pán-ta é-nas pý-rau-los sto pá-rty tis yei-to-ni-ás.)

969. Attending the local cultural fair is a tradition.
Η επίσκεψη στην τοπική πολιτιστική έκθεση είναι παράδοση.
(I e-pí-skep-si stin to-pi-kí po-li-ti-sti-kí ék-the-si eí-nai pa-rá-do-si.)

970. I'm thrilled to be part of the community celebration.
Είμαι ενθουσιασμένος που είμαι μέρος της κοινοτικής γιορτής.
(Eí-mai en-thou-si-as-mé-nos pou eí-mai mé-ros tis koi-no-ti-kís yior-tís.)

971. The music and dancing at the wedding were fantastic.
Η μουσική και ο χορός στον γάμο ήταν φανταστικοί.
(I mou-si-kí kai o cho-rós ston gá-mo í-tan fan-tas-ti-koí.)

972. Let's join the festivities at the holiday parade.
Ας συμμετάσχουμε στις εορταστικές εκδηλώσεις της παρέλασης.
(As sym-me-tá-schou-me stis eor-tas-ti-kés ek-di-ló-seis tis pa-ré-la-sis.)

973. The cultural exchange event was enlightening.
Η εκδήλωση πολιτιστικής ανταλλαγής ήταν διαφωτιστική.
(I ek-dí-lo-si po-li-ti-sti-kís an-ta-la-gís í-tan di-a-fo-ti-sti-kí.)

974. The food at the international festival was delicious.
Το φαγητό στο διεθνές φεστιβάλ ήταν νόστιμο.
(To fa-yi-tó sto di-e-thnés fes-ti-vál í-tan nó-sti-mo.)

> **Travel Story:** In a spice shop in Heraklion, the owner said, "Κάθε μπαχαρικό έχει τη μαγεία του," translating to "Every spice has its magic," emphasizing their flavors and aromas.

75. I had a great time at the costume party.
Πέρασα υπέροχα στο πάρτι μεταμφιέσεων.
(Pé-ra-sa y-pé-ro-cha sto pá-rti me-ta-mfié-seon.)

76. Let's toast to a memorable evening!
Ας αναστήσουμε για μια αξέχαστη βραδιά!
(As a-na-stí-sou-me gia mi-a axé-chas-ti vra-di-á!)

77. The concert was a musical extravaganza.
Η συναυλία ήταν μουσικό εξτραβαγκάντζα.
(I sy-na-vli-á í-tan mou-si-kó ex-tra-va-gán-tza.)

78. I'm looking forward to the art exhibition.
Ανυπομονώ για την έκθεση τέχνης.
(A-ni-po-mo-nó gia tin ék-the-si téch-nis.)

79. The theater performance was outstanding.
Η θεατρική παράσταση ήταν εξαιρετική.
(I the-a-tri-kí pa-rás-ta-si í-tan ex-ai-re-ti-kí.)

80. We should participate in the charity fundraiser.
Πρέπει να συμμετέχουμε στην φιλανθρωπική εκδήλωση.
(Pré-pei na sym-me-té-chou-me stin fi-lan-thro-pi-kí ek-dí-lo-si.)

81. The sports tournament was thrilling to watch.
Ο αθλητικός τουρνουά ήταν συναρπαστικό να παρακολουθήσεις.
(O ath-li-ti-kós tour-nou-á í-tan sy-nar-pas-ti-kó na pa-ra-ko-lou-thí-seis.)

82. Let's embrace the local customs and traditions.
Ας αγκαλιάσουμε τα τοπικά έθιμα και τις παραδόσεις.
(As an-ga-liá-sou-me ta to-pi-ká é-thi-ma kai tis pa-rá-do-seis.)

Giving and Receiving Gifts

983. I hope you like this gift I got for you.
Ελπίζω να σου αρέσει αυτό το δώρο που σου πήρα.
(El-pí-zo na sou a-ré-sei af-tó to dó-ro pou sou pí-ra.)

984. Thank you for the thoughtful present!
Ευχαριστώ για το σκεπτόμενο δώρο!
(Ef-cha-ri-stó gia to skep-tó-me-no dó-ro!)

985. It's a token of my appreciation.
Είναι ένα δείγμα της εκτίμησής μου.
(Í-ne é-na díg-ma tis ek-tí-mi-sís mou.)

986. Here's a little something to brighten your day.
Ιδού κάτι μικρό για να φωτίσει τη μέρα σου.
(I-dú ká-ti mi-kró gia na fo-tí-sei ti mé-ra sou.)

987. I brought you a souvenir from my trip.
Σου έφερα ένα αναμνηστικό από το ταξίδι μου.
(Sou é-fe-ra é-na a-na-mni-sti-kó apó to ta-xí-di mou.)

988. This gift is for you on your special day.
Αυτό το δώρο είναι για εσένα για την ξεχωριστή σου μέρα.
(Af-tó to dó-ro í-ne gia e-sé-na gia tin xe-cho-ri-stí sou mé-ra.)

989. I got this with you in mind.
Αυτό το πήρα έχοντας εσένα στο μυαλό μου.
(Af-tó to pí-ra é-chon-tas e-sé-na sto my-a-ló mou.)

90. You shouldn't have, but I love it!
Δεν έπρεπε, αλλά το αγαπώ!
(Den é-pre-pe, al-lá to a-ga-pó!)

91. It's a small gesture of my gratitude.
Είναι ένας μικρός χειρονομία της ευγνωμοσύνης μου.
(Í-ne é-nas mi-krós chei-ro-no-mía tis ef-gno-mo-sý-nis mou.)

92. I wanted to give you a little surprise.
Ήθελα να σου δώσω μια μικρή έκπληξη.
(Í-the-la na sou dó-so mi-a mi-krí ék-pli-xi.)

93. I hope this gift brings you joy.
Ελπίζω αυτό το δώρο να σου φέρει χαρά.
(El-pí-zo af-tó to dó-ro na sou fé-rei cha-rá.)

94. It's a symbol of our friendship.
Είναι ένα σύμβολο της φιλίας μας.
(Í-ne é-na sým-vo-lo tis fi-lí-as mas.)

95. This is just a token of my love.
Είναι απλώς ένα δείγμα της αγάπης μου.
(Í-ne ap-lós é-na deíg-ma tis a-gá-pis mou.)

96. I knew you'd appreciate this.
Ήξερα ότι θα το εκτιμήσεις.
(Í-xe-ra ó-ti tha to ek-ti-mí-seis.)

97. I wanted to spoil you a bit.
Ήθελα να σε κακομάθω λίγο.
(Í-the-la na se ka-ko-má-tho lí-go.)

998. This gift is for your hard work.
Αυτό το δώρο είναι για την σκληρή σου δουλειά.
(Af-tó to dó-ro eí-nai gia tin skli-rí sou dou-lei-á.)

999. I hope you find this useful.
Ελπίζω να το βρεις χρήσιμο.
(El-pí-zo na to vreís chrí-si-mo.)

1000. It's a sign of my affection.
Είναι ένα σημάδι της αγάπης μου.
(Eí-nai é-na si-má-di tis a-gá-pis mou.)

1001. I brought you a little memento.
Σου έφερα ένα μικρό αναμνηστικό.
(Sou é-fe-ra é-na mi-kró a-na-mni-sti-kó.)

> "Ουδέν κακόν αμιγές καλού."
> **"There is nothing bad without something good."**
> *In every bad situation, there can be a positive aspect or outcome.*

Interactive Challenge: Special Occasions
(Link each English word with their corresponding meaning in Greek)

1) Celebration	Έκπληξη
2) Gift	Χαιρετισμός
3) Party	Πρόποση
4) Anniversary	Εορταστικός
5) Congratulations	Επέτειος
6) Wedding	Παράδοση
7) Birthday	Δώρο
8) Graduation	Γενέθλια
9) Holiday	Συγχαρητήρια
10) Ceremony	Εορτασμός
11) Tradition	Γάμος
12) Festive	Πάρτι
13) Greeting	Τελετή
14) Toast	Διακοπές
15) Surprise	Αποφοίτηση

Correct Answers:

1. Celebration - Εορτασμός
2. Gift - Δώρο
3. Party - Πάρτι
4. Anniversary - Επέτειος
5. Congratulations - Συγχαρητήρια
6. Wedding - Γάμος
7. Birthday - Γενέθλια
8. Graduation - Αποφοίτηση
9. Holiday - Διακοπές
10. Ceremony - Τελετή
11. Tradition - Παράδοση
12. Festive - Εορταστικός
13. Greeting - Χαιρετισμός
14. Toast - Πρόποση
15. Surprise - Έκπληξη

CONCLUSION

Congratulations on reaching the final chapter of "The Ultimate Greek Phrase Book." As you set out to immerse yourself in the rich and ancient culture of Greece, from the awe-inspiring Acropolis of Athens the idyllic beaches of the Greek islands, your commitment to mastering Greek is truly commendable.

This phrasebook has been your steadfast companion, providing you with key phrases and expressions to enhance your communication with ease. You've progressed from simple greetings like "Γειά σου" (Yiá sou) and "Καλημέρα" (Kaliméra) to more complex sentences, equipping you for engaging conversations, unforgettable experiences, and a deeper connection with Greece's illustrious history.

Embarking on the journey to language proficiency is a rewarding pursuit. Your dedication has built a solid foundation for fluency in Greek. Remember, language is more than a means of communication; it's a bridge to understanding the soul and traditions of a culture.

If this phrasebook has contributed to your language learning adventure I would love to hear about it! Connect with me on Instagram: **@adriangruszka**. Share your stories, ask for advice, or just drop a "Γειά σου!" I'd be thrilled if you mention this book on social media and tag me – I'm eager to celebrate your advancements in mastering Greek.

For further resources, detailed insights, and updates, please visit **www.adriangee.com**. There, you'll discover a treasure trove of information, including recommended courses and a community of fellow language learners ready to support your continuous journey.

Learning a new language opens doors to new friendships and viewpoints. Your enthusiasm for learning and adapting is your greatest asset in this linguistic adventure. Embrace every chance to learn, interact, and deepen your understanding of Greek culture and life.

Καλή τύχη! (Good luck!) Continue to practice with dedication, refine your skills, and most importantly, enjoy every moment of your Greek language journey.

Σας ευχαριστώ πολύ! (Thank you very much!) for choosing this phrasebook. May your future endeavors be enriched with meaningful exchanges and achievements as you delve deeper into the captivating world of languages!

Adrian Gee

Made in United States
Troutdale, OR
01/31/2024

17336560R00148